the
SUPERNATURAL
PRAYER *of* JESUS

the
SUPERNATURAL
PRAYER *of* JESUS

Prayer Secrets from the Son of God that
Unleash the Miracle Realm

CHAD GONZALES

DESTINY IMAGE® PUBLISHERS, INC.

P.O. Box 310, Shippensburg, PA 17257-0310

"Promoting Inspired Lives."

This book and all other Destiny Image and Destiny Image Fiction books are available at Christian bookstores and distributors worldwide.

For more information on foreign distributors, call 717-532-3040.

Reach us on the Internet: www.destinyimage.com.

ISBN 13 TP: 978-0-7684-6380-4
ISBN 13 eBook: 978-0-7684-6381-1

For Worldwide Distribution, Printed in the U.S.A.
2 3 4 5 6 7 8 / 27 26 25 24 23

CONTENTS

Introduction

Our Father in heaven. Hallowed be Your Name. Your kingdom come, Your will be done on earth as it is in heaven (Matthew 6:9–10).

Most Christians and even many sinners know the words in our opening verse. These famous words are the beginning of what many in the world know as "The Lord's Prayer."

In Matthew 6, we find the disciples asking Jesus how to pray, and what we know as the Lord's Prayer was the example Jesus gave them when He said:

In this manner, therefore, pray: Our Father in heaven, hallowed be Your name. Your kingdom come. Your will be done on earth as it is in heaven. Give us this day our daily bread. And forgive us our debts, as we forgive our debtors. And do not lead us into temptation, but deliver us from the evil one. For Yours is the kingdom and the power and the glory forever. Amen (Matthew 6:9–13).

There have been countless sermons and books teaching, dissecting, and expounding on the Lord's Prayer. I've seen the prayer posted in churches, funeral homes, and hospitals; I have even heard it prayed before sporting events.

As wonderful as this prayer is, there is another prayer Jesus prayed that we have on record. In John 17, we find Jesus praying in the upper room right before His betrayal and arrest in the garden of Gethsemane. Unfortunately, the only thing people know about this time was that Jesus and the disciples were sitting around a table and having the Last Supper.

Although we know Jesus spent numerous hours in prayer with the Father, this prayer is the only time we get to hear exactly what was said in one of Jesus' actual prayer times. In my opinion, THIS is the Lord's prayer, and you find the substance of Matthew 6:9–13 in Jesus' prayer in the upper room, except it is expanded upon and filled with life-changing, new covenant truths. Jesus' prayer in Matthew 6 was an old covenant prayer; Jesus' prayer in John 17 was a prophetic, new covenant prayer founded in grace and union with the Father. If there ever was a prayer in the Bible to be preached, taught, dissected, and expounded upon, it is the High Priestly Prayer of Jesus found in John 17:

> *Jesus spoke these words, lifted up His eyes to heaven, and said: "Father, the hour has come. Glorify Your Son, that Your Son also may glorify You, as You have given Him authority over all flesh, that He should give eternal life to as many as You have given Him. And this is eternal life, that they may know You, the only true God, and Jesus Christ whom*

You have sent. I have glorified You on the earth. I have finished the work which You have given Me to do. And now, O Father, glorify Me together with Yourself, with the glory which I had with You before the world was. I have manifested Your name to the men whom You have given Me out of the world. They were Yours, You gave them to Me, and they have kept Your word. Now they have known that all things which You have given Me are from You. For I have given to them the words which You have given Me; and they have received them, and have known surely that I came forth from You; and they have believed that You sent Me. I pray for them. I do not pray for the world but for those whom You have given Me, for they are Yours. And all Mine are Yours, and Yours are Mine, and I am glorified in them. Now I am no longer in the world, but these are in the world, and I come to You. Holy Father, keep through Your name those whom You have given Me, that they may be one as We are. While I was with them in the world, I kept them in Your name. Those whom You gave Me I have kept; and none of them is lost except the son of perdition, that the Scripture might be fulfilled. But now I come to You, and these things I speak in the world, that they may have My joy fulfilled in themselves. I have given them Your word; and the world has hated them because they are not of the world, just as I am not of the world. I do not pray that You should take them out of the world, but that You should keep them from the evil one. They are not of the world, just as I am not of the world. Sanctify them by Your truth. Your word is truth. As You sent Me into the world, I also have sent them into the world. And for their sakes I sanctify Myself, that they also may be sanctified by the truth. I do not pray for these alone, but also for those who will believe in Me through their word; that they all may *be one, as You, Father, are in Me, and I in You; that they also may be one in Us, that the world may believe that You sent Me. And the glory which You gave Me I have given them, that they may be one just as We are one: I in them, and You in Me; that they may be made perfect in one, and that the world may know that You have sent Me, and have loved them as You have loved Me. Father, I desire that they also whom You gave Me may be with Me where I am, that they may behold My glory which You have given Me; for You loved Me before the foundation of the world. O righteous Father! The world has not known You, but I have known You; and these have known that You sent Me. And I have declared to them Your name, and will declare it, that the love with which You loved Me may be in them, and I in them."*

I am so thankful the Holy Spirit gave us this prayer. Not only do we see the heart of Jesus and His commitment to the plan of God, but we also discover priceless truths regarding our union and identity with Christ. In this prayer, we find Jesus declaring many of the wonderful, redemptive realities that He would later reveal to the apostle Paul, and as a result, they're given to us in the Pauline Epistles. In reality, Jesus prophetically prayed out the entire Christian experience.

In this prayer, we discover the purpose of salvation from the beginning to the end. Jesus prayed out our purpose for being on the earth, our position and fellowship with the Father, healing, financial prosperity, supernatural protection, supernatural encounters, and eventually our physically being with Him once again.

Jesus' prayer in John 17 is amazing and filled with nuggets of revelation. In verses 1–8, we find Jesus talking to God about Himself. Jesus revealed His purpose for coming to the earth and the true meaning of eternal life. Jesus also petitioned God to restore to Him the greater glory He had before He came to the earth. In Philippians 2:7–8, the apostle Paul said that Jesus laid aside the glory He had in Heaven when coming to the earth. We know that Jesus walked as a man anointed by God, so this reveals the glory Jesus walked in on the earth was less than what He had in Heaven (see Acts 10:38). If Jesus came to take Adam's place as a man, then He would have to walk in the same anointing Adam had as a man.

In verses 9–26, we find Jesus talking to God about us. It is in this passage that we basically find a concise summary of what the Christian experience is all about. Thank God, we have the Epistles, but if all we had was Jesus' prayer in John 17, we would have the starting point for understanding (1) redemption, (2) the staggering reality of our union with Christ, and (3) the foundation for living a supernatural life on the earth.

I have spent the better part of the last eighteen years studying and meditating on the words Jesus prayed and am continuing to grasp at these marvelous truths. There are truths in this prayer we must grab hold of so that we can walk in the fullness of God in us and represent Him with perfection to the world.

Jesus' prayer in John 17 reveals the heartbeat of Jesus and the plan of God for our lives under the covenant of grace. I personally believe the words Jesus prayed in John 17 were the most important words

Jesus spoke on the earth. The teaching we find in John 13–16 took place in the upper room and is filled with the deepest teachings Jesus gave regarding union with God, the love of God, and the Holy Spirit's working in our lives. Jesus crowned these last moments with the disciples by praying and prophetically declaring new creation realities that had been in the heart of the Father before the foundation of the world.

Jesus came to the earth not only to die for us, but to pray this prayer for us. This was Jesus praying out the will of God so that God could perform His Word!

Jesus always gets His prayers answered, and John 17 was answered as well. The things Jesus prayed were of the utmost importance to Him, and if they were important to Him, they need to be important to us. Legally, this prayer was fulfilled and provided for all; however, just as with salvation and all the realities of redemption, we must lay hold of these realities and renew our minds to them so they can be real in our lives.

I'm still in awe that in over two thousand years, very little has been taught on this prayer. However, I believe in this last, great move of God on the earth, the true sons and daughters of God will finally walk in the fullness of what Jesus prayed—not because God was holding out, but because we dared to expand our souls and, by faith, see ourselves the way God sees us in Christ.

Uniting man and God again was at the forefront of Jesus' thoughts. This purpose of unification propelled Him on the earth so that the life of God would once again flow in and through man, and fellowship with God would be completely restored.

The High Priestly Prayer of Jesus was a supernatural, prophetic prayer for us. In the Old Testament, we see that one of the responsibilities of the High Priest was to pray to God on behalf of the people. Just as the priests of the old covenant did for the people, Jesus was doing for us. As we go through this supernatural prayer of Jesus for us, allow the Holy Spirit to give you fresh revelation and insight into every request that Jesus made of the Father. May every prayer that we pray open our eyes to our union with Christ. May we understand all that He has done for us, all that He is doing in us, and all He is endeavoring to do through us.

Chapter 1

"I Pray for Them"

I pray for them. I do not pray for the world but for those whom You have given Me, for they are Yours (John 17:9).

It's staggering to think that as Jesus was hours away from being brutally beaten and tortured, He was praying for me and praying for you. Jesus would not only be tortured physically, but He was taunted by the demonic forces of hell. One can only imagine the jeers, the insults and foul things being flung his way from satan's army. King David saw into the spirit and prophetically declared the sufferings of Christ in Psalm 22.

I'm surrounded by many violent foes like bulls; forces of evil encircle me like the strong bulls of Bashan. Like ravenous, roaring lions tearing their prey, they pour curses from their mouths. Now I'm completely exhausted. Every joint of my body has been pulled apart. My courage has melted away. I'm so thirsty and parched. My tongue sticks to the roof of my mouth. And now you lay me in the dust of death. They have pierced my hands and my feet. Like a pack of wild dogs they tear at me, swirling around me with their hatred. A band of evil men surrounds me. I can count all my bones. Look at how they gloat over me and stare! (vv. 12–17 TPT).

Jesus knew what awaited Him. He knew the physical torture of the cross. He knew the spiritual torment that was coming His way. Jesus knew the ultimate punishment would be the separation from the Father, and through that sweat mingled with blood began to ooze out His pores. Despite what lay ahead of Jesus, we were on His mind.

Jesus knew that the disciples were His responsibility. Why? Because the disciples were God's property, but He had given them to Jesus not only to be their Shepherd, but also to be God's steward over them.

Right here we see the vitally important role of the pastor at work. My wife, Lacy, and I started two churches and pastored for fifteen years. I know what it is like to see people come and go. I know what it is like to have church members come to you with life and death situations. I know what it is like being alerted by the Holy Spirit and spending hours praying in the Spirit for a church member going through an attack.

In my fifteen years as a pastor, I took my position seriously. I understood the authority I had in the lives of those who had submitted themselves to me. As a result, I never had a church member die of a disease in all our fifteen years of pastoring. I have done many funerals over the years, but in fifteen years, I only conducted two funerals that were for my own people: one died of old age and the other died of a stress-induced heart attack in the middle of the night. There is a level of authority available to the pastor that I don't think we have realized. If we were walking in this revelation, there would be more honor given to the pastor by the people in their respective churches. The people wouldn't get so easily offended and leave because they didn't get their way.

Most Christians don't realize that when God sends them to a church, it is not only because they have a God-given supply for that church, but also God has a God-given supply for them through their pastor and the other members of the body there.

Jesus took His responsibility of caring for, protecting, and growing the disciples very seriously. He recognized that He was the steward of God's property, and because the disciples were God's property, they were extremely valuable. We will see later on that Jesus was able to intercede on behalf of those who were submitted to Him. The one to whom you submit yourself becomes your master!

While Jesus was praying in the upper room, He was not only preparing to step into His role as our Savior, He was also preparing to step into His role as our great High Priest and Intercessor! Jesus was praying for us then and is still praying for us now as Hebrews 7:24–25 tells us:

> *But Jesus permanently holds his priestly office, since he lives forever and will never have a successor! So he is able to save fully from now throughout eternity, everyone who comes to God through him, because he lives to pray continually for them* (TPT).

We all have been in hard times and longed for someone to pray for us. However, even if we couldn't find anyone, how wonderful it has been to know that Jesus has been praying for us. In fact, Jesus lives to pray continually for us! Think about the times you have asked someone to pray for you and how it brought some measure of comfort. It has always meant the world to me when I hear some of our partners tell us what and how they have been praying for us. Occasionally, I may receive a text from friends letting me know they are praying for me. I don't know about you, but that blesses me! Yet, how much more should it bless us and encourage us that *Jesus is always praying for us?*

Jesus lives to pray for us. Jesus as our Intercessor is not just a job title or responsibility; it is something He lives to do. The word *lives* is the Greek word *zao* and means to be full of vigor, fresh, strong, powerful, and efficient. This isn't talking about a weak prayer of pity someone says for you. This is talking about someone who is effective and efficient in their praying, like a skilled carpenter who knows how to use his tools. Jesus knows how to pray and get results!

Praying for you is something Jesus wants to do because He loves you and wants to see you fulfill the call of God on your life. He wants to see you prosper in everything that you do. This truth alone should make us take a deep sigh and experience peace even in the midst of the perfect storm! Despite the giants standing in front of you, you should stand tall with a soul full of boldness, knowing that Jesus is praying for your triumph. As the apostle Paul said,

> *Who then is left to condemn us? Certainly not Jesus, the Anointed One! For he gave his life for us, and even more than that he has*

conquered death and is now risen, exalted,
and enthroned by God at his right hand.
so how could he possibly condemn us since
he is continually praying for our triumph?
(Romans 8:34 TPT).

Jesus has already won the victory for us. We simply need to be strong in Him and walk it out. In those times when you start to feel weak, stop for a moment and remind yourself that the greatest Intercessor of all is praying for you right then. He is personally representing you to the Father. Jesus knows what you feel and knows what you are going through; He has been there and done that! Jesus was praying for you in the upper room, and He is now praying for you in Heaven!

Now, this is where our praying can get fun and produce great results. Wouldn't you like to get results when you pray? Well, what if we started praying on Earth what Jesus was praying in Heaven? Is that possible? Certainly!

Right before Jesus began to pray in the upper room, He gave the disciples a tremendous teaching about union. During this time of the Last Supper, Jesus went into His role of prayer in our lives. Jesus said,

> *I am the sprouting vine and you're my branches. as you live in union with me as your source, fruitfulness will stream from within you—but when you live separated from me you are powerless. If a person is separated from me, he is discarded; such branches are gathered up and thrown into the fire to be burned. But if you live in life-union with me and if my words live powerfully within you—then you can ask whatever you desire and it will be done. When your lives bear abundant fruit, you demonstrate that you are my mature disciples who glorify my Father!* (John 15:5–8 TPT).

Notice verse 7, where Jesus said, "*If you live in life union with me and my words live powerfully within you, then you can ask whatever you desire and it will be done.*" This points to part of Jesus' role in praying for us. Through our union with Him, His words can flow powerfully through us. The Holy Spirit can reveal to us the words of Jesus in which to pray and ultimately produce great results. Not only is Jesus praying for us, when we pray what He prays, we will experience tremendous fruit on the earth. Jesus will come into agreement with us in our prayers.

There is another truth to this that I think we have missed out on. During one of Jesus' teaching times with the disciples, He gave another revelation concerning His role with us in prayer. He said,

> *Receive this truth: Whatever you forbid on earth will be considered to be forbidden in heaven, and whatever you release on earth will be considered to be released in heaven. Again, I give you an eternal truth: If two of you agree to ask God for something in a symphony of prayer, my heavenly Father will do it for you. For wherever two or three come together in honor of my name, I am right there with them!* (Matthew 18:18–20 TPT).

Jesus said that in our time of prayer, He is right there in the middle of it! Jesus unites with us in prayer to bring what we have asked to pass—talk about a prayer partner!

Friend, know that Jesus lives to pray for you. If there is ever a time in which you start to get down and think you are all alone, look at Jesus in the upper room. Look at what He said: *"Father, I pray for those You gave Me."* You are the personal property of Jesus Christ, and one of His responsibilities as High Priest is to continually pray for you. There may be times when it looks like you have a fight on your hands, and no one is in your corner—but rest assured—Jesus is there! Jesus is interceding on your behalf for your victory, and He is there to come into agreement with you concerning the desires of your heart.

PRAYER

Father, thank You that You gave Jesus to not only be my Savior, but also to be my personal Intercessor. Jesus, thank You for praying for me; I draw strength from Your prayers, and by faith, I come into agreement with what

You are praying. Holy Spirit, I ask You to reveal to me how to align my prayers with Jesus so that I pray what He prays.

Chapter 2

"I Am Glorified in Them"

And all Mine are Yours, and
Yours are Mine, and I am
glorified in them (John 17:10).

There are far too many Christians who have a low self-image of themselves. Why is that? Because too many of us allow our self-worth to be determined by those around us. Television commercials and online ads show the current trends of which we too often measure ourselves against only to find out the next day those trends have changed.

We also live in a very loveless world in which worth can be based on skin color, race, or wealth. I remember, when I was in middle school, I was bullied by some simply because of my last name. I was called racially insensitive names, and physical fights were started because of it. Unfortunately, being bullied followed me to college. I was on the basketball team, and during my sophomore year, we had a tournament during the Christmas break. The tournament was to be held in Wisconsin, and I was really excited about going because I had never been to too many places outside of Texas. I grew up in a poor family; as a result, our vacations were usually a few days in Galveston, Texas, which was only about forty-five minutes away. So, I was excited at the opportunity to visit some other states up north! But my excitement was short-lived when my coach called me to his office and informed me that I couldn't go. He didn't tell me why, but he did let me know it wasn't his decision.

I was heartbroken. While my teammates were getting ready for the basketball trip, I began the five-hour drive to my parents' house in Beaumont, Texas. I was so upset that I didn't even bother to stick around for our team picture for that year. I almost quit the team over it all but decided to stick it out for the remainder of the year. It was later on that I found out the athletic director had a problem with me because I was Hispanic.

Many of us have had circumstances in life where because of our race, economic status, or family history or background, we didn't fit in; as a result, we didn't feel of any value or worth. There were many times I could have let my economic status and the racial issues define me—but I was just too hardheaded. I have always been a fighter, so I chose not to let those things get me down; however, when I began to understand how God saw me, I began to get a massive boost in my sense of self-worth.

In John 17:10, Jesus said, *"All Mine are Yours, and Yours are Mine."* Do you think God owns junk? Certainly not. We can see in Genesis 1 that when God was creating the world, it was good; yet, when He created man, it was more than good—because man was created in the image of God! God modeled man after Himself. When God made man, He made man to be perfect because God took of Himself and made Adam.

Sadly, Adam sinned and died spiritually. He lost out on the union of God and the life of God, but thankfully, Jesus came to get these back for us. Because of salvation, you and I become one with Christ, and He becomes one with us. When we are born again, we are made of the very same substance of God, and because of that we are of tremendous value.

Now, let's take this a giant step further. If you have ever wondered if you are special, look at what Jesus said as He was praying to the Father: *"I am glorified in them."* The word *glorified* in the Greek means "to cause the dignity and worth of some person or thing to become manifest and acknowledged."[1]

Think about this: The worth of Jesus is seen through you! That's a mind-blowing statement. It's one thing to know you are valuable; it's quite another to know the value of Jesus can be seen and experienced through you. There isn't a price tag that can be put on you because you are priceless.

In Christ, God made you so unique that you can exhibit the qualities of Christ. God empowered you with the very same power that flows in Jesus. The grace that was upon Jesus to reveal the Father is the same grace upon you to reveal the Christ.

Friend, this goes so much further than following rules and trying to be a better person; this is about representing Jesus in His fullness!

If we take a look at the disciples that were with Jesus in the upper room, it becomes quickly evident Jesus was not referring to their character, personality, or physical makeup. The disciples were a band of misfits before they met Jesus. Among those on the Jesus Christ Evangelistic Team were Matthew, who was a callous tax collector; Judas, who was a heartless thief; James and John, who were only concerned about titles and power; and Peter, who had a horrible temper.

I'm still amazed at the patience of Jesus throughout His time with the Twelve; there had to be lots of "Are you kidding Me?" moments for Jesus! Despite their immaturity, there was one thing that I see in the disciples that still hasn't been matched by much of the modern Church: They took the power and authority Jesus gave them and replicated Him.

> *Jesus summoned together his twelve apostles and imparted to them authority over every demon and the power to heal every disease. Then he commissioned them to proclaim God's kingdom and to heal the sick to demonstrate that the kingdom had arrived. As he sent them out, he gave them these instructions: "Take nothing extra on your journey. Just go as you are. Don't carry a staff, a backpack, food, money, not even a change of clothes. Whatever home welcomes you as a guest, remain there and make it your base of ministry. And wherever your ministry is rejected, you are to leave that town and shake the dust off your shoes as a testimony before them." The apostles departed and went into the villages with the wonderful news of God's kingdom, and they healed diseases wherever they went* (Luke 9:1–6 TPT).

When the disciples went out preaching the Kingdom, casting out demons, and healing the sick, Jesus was being glorified, and God was being glorified. Despite their personality flaws and issues of immaturity, they were still getting results like Jesus. You will find that with God, it is not about what you know but about what you produce. God wants you to produce fruit with the supernatural power and authority He has given you. That's why Jesus said,

> *I am the sprouting vine and you're my branches. As you live in union with Me as your source, fruitfulness will stream from within you—but when you live separated from me you are powerless. If a person is separated from me, he is discarded; such branches are gathered up and thrown into the fire to be burned. But if you live in life-union with me and if my words live powerfully within you—then you can ask whatever you desire and it will be done. When your lives bear abundant fruit, you demonstrate that*

you are my mature disciples who glorify my Father! (John 15:5–8 TPT).

Notice that through our union with Christ, we can speak what Jesus speaks and manifest Heaven. Through our union with Christ, fruit is produced, and He gets glory! We should have high morals and live lives full of integrity and honor, but this is not the type of fruit Jesus was talking about. Sinners can choose to live lives of honor, but they can't produce supernatural fruit from Heaven! Through our union with Christ, His words can flow through us, and we can act in His place on the earth. As a result, the great honor and value of God are shown in you!

Jesus said that because of our union with Him, God has given us access to anything Heaven has to offer. When the goodness of God is produced in us and through us, the value of Jesus and the value of God are on display!

The next time you look in the mirror, remind yourself of how valuable you are because of Jesus. You're not only valuable because He died for you, but you are also valuable because people can see Him or His value in you.

Are you ready to take this even further? You and Jesus share the same value! You are just as valuable to God as Jesus is valuable to God. How could the dignity, value, and worth of Jesus be seen in you if you didn't share it to the same degree? When people see you, they should see the Christ!

How many times have you heard the statement, "You may be the only Jesus people see." Well, it is a very true statement, but again, it goes far beyond being a good person. If the world is going to see the goodness of God, they will have to see it through you. They need to see you prospering in every area of your life. The world needs to see extraordinary differences in your relationships, finances, and health than its own. The world needs to see the light shining in your life while all the world is filled with darkness. While the economy is tanking, the world needs to see you prospering. While the world is experiencing a health pandemic, they need to see you experiencing divine health. What does this do? It brings Jesus glory through you.

There should never be a Christian with a self-esteem problem. There should never be a Christian with a self-worth problem. You are of high value because you are a child of the King. Certainly, there are people who are born in this world with a greater head start than others, but you must understand that when you become one with Christ, that position becomes the great equalizer. You may have had less of a head start than others in the world, but when you become His, He will not only catch you up, but take you further than you ever could have imagined.

Don't ever forget that you are His.

PRAYER

Father, I ask You to open my eyes and help me to see how You see me. Jesus, thank You for entrusting me with Your authority and power here on the earth so I could bring You glory. Holy Spirit, I will follow You everywhere You lead. I will only say what I hear

You say and only do what I see You do so that people see the dignity, worth, and value of Christ through me.

Chapter 3

"That They May Be One as We Are One"

Now I am no longer in the world, but these are in the world, and I come to You. Holy Father, keep through Your name those whom You have given Me, that they may be one as We are (John 17:11).

As Jesus prayed in the upper room, Jesus had already made a shift in perspective. Although He was sitting there among the disciples praying, Jesus declared He was already out of this world; in His heart, the coming days were already done. Jesus had just one last thing to do to fulfill His purpose, and then He would go home to be with the Father. Over the next few days, Jesus would not be there physically to protect His disciples. Jesus would not be there to exert dominion over satan and to keep the disciples protected in prayer; as a result, Jesus turned them over to the Father for protection.

Jesus had a serious task at hand, and He wanted to make sure that all those whom God had given Him would share in the reward of His obedience. Most Christians would assume the reward was that of going to Heaven, but was that truly the ultimate reward? Look at what Jesus said, *"Holy Father, keep through Your name those whom You have given Me that they may be one as We are."*

For centuries, we have heard that Jesus came so we could go to Heaven. Certainly, there is a Heaven and a hell. Hell was made for satan and his demonic forces; unfortunately, those who do not receive Jesus as their Lord and Savior will go to hell because they chose to stay aligned with satan.

One of the benefits of salvation is that we get to go to Heaven; however, if the only reason for salvation was so we could go to Heaven, then why are we still here after we accept Jesus? The answer is simple: Jesus didn't come to change your destination; Jesus came to change your position. The primary focus of Jesus' ministry was not to take you somewhere, but to get Someone in you! Jesus came to unite you with God! The purpose of salvation was to unite man and God together again. Thankfully, when we take our last breath on this earth, we get to be in Heaven with Jesus, but that is not when life gets good.

I remember, when I was a kid, we used to sing in church, "When we all get to Heaven, what a day of rejoicing that will be!" The focus of the salvation experience was always on the future, but friend, God cares about your "now"! We should be experiencing the good life now!

Jesus told us in John 10:10 that He came to give us life and life more abundantly. Notice again, Jesus did not say, "I came so you could go to Heaven." Was going to Heaven part of the salvation package? Yes, but it was not the primary focus.

Friend, satan has no problem with you focusing on "when we all get to Heaven." It is certainly something to be excited about, but getting to Heaven is not my focus; manifesting Heaven on earth is my focus!

As long as you think your victory is in your future, you'll continue to live defeated in your now. This explains why so many Christians look at death as the real answer for their problems; they don't really want to die, but they truly see it as the end of all their problems. Most Christians look at death as the answer for sickness and disease! Friend, if death were your savior for sickness and disease, then why did Jesus die for your sickness? Is Jesus your Healer, or is death your healer? You don't need to die and go to Heaven to be free of disease; you can get saved and experience freedom from disease here on the earth. Yet many Christians are living life waiting to get to Heaven while they go through hell on earth.

I remember as a kid in church, watching all the people go up to the altar at the end of church service. Many would be up there on their knees, crying and wailing; others would be around them, consoling them and crying with them. I'm not trying to be critical, but this was at the end of every service! The same people, the same tears, and the same lack of victory in their life. It was depressing! That was the saddest bunch of Christians I was ever around; no wonder they stayed sick and broke! I'm sure Jesus was in Heaven shaking His head in frustration while satan was laughing until his cheeks hurt.

These people at my church were sweet people but had no idea as to what Jesus had already done for them. They were all at the altar crying for victory—not realizing Jesus had already been to the altar for their victory. It was only later in life that I found out you could leave church with a sense of victory rather than defeat.

Notice also that Jesus said, *"I came to give."* Jesus came to give you something, not just take you somewhere! Jesus came to give you life! This word *life* is the Greek word *zoe*, which the *Strong's Concordance* defines as "the absolute fulness of life which belongs to God."[2] I simply define *zoe* as "the life that God is and the life that God has." Jesus came to give you the very same life that flows in Him and flows in God.

In John 5:26, Jesus said, *"For as the Father has life in Himself, so He has granted the Son to have life in Himself."* The life the Father has is the same life the Son has; through our union with Christ, that same life is now in us—to affect our spirits and to bring healing to our bodies.

The life Jesus gave us not only put us in the position to walk in divine health, but it also gave us the same substance, the same life, that fills God Himself. This put us in a position to walk with Him, talk with Him, and experience Him on His level.

In John 17:3, Jesus said, *"Eternal life means to know and experience you as the only true God and to know and experience Jesus Christ, as the Son whom you have sent"* (TPT).

Jesus didn't say eternal life was about going to Heaven; Jesus said eternal life was about an experiential knowledge of God. Salvation put you in a position so that you could experience God on a regular basis!

When Jesus was talking to the Twelve in the upper room, He talked to them about this very thing.

Soon I will leave this world and they will see Me no longer, but you will see Me, because I will live again, and you will come alive too. So when that day comes, you will know that I am living in the Father and that you are one with me, for I will be living in you. Those who truly love me are those who obey my commands. whoever passionately loves me will be passionately loved by my Father. And I will passionately love him in return and will reveal myself to him (John 14:19–21 TPT).

Jesus said that on the day of salvation, you would know He is in the Father, and you are in Jesus, and He is in you. The word *know* is the Greek word *ginosko*, which means "to become acquainted with or to understand."[3] It is also a Jewish idiom for an intimate relationship between a man and woman; as a result, we can see this is not talking about simply knowing facts but having knowledge by experience. Jesus was not simply talking about you having factual knowledge about your union with God; Jesus was talking about an experiential knowledge about your union with God where you walk with Him, talk with Him, and seek Him!

Jesus continued and said, *"And I will passionately love him in return and reveal myself to him."* Notice Jesus didn't say, "I will take him to Heaven!" Jesus was letting you know that on the day of salvation, you should begin experiencing Him! Salvation was more than just opening the door to Heaven; it was about opening the door to Him.

As Jesus sat in the upper room praying, the cord that ran through His prayer was God once again uniting with man. United man with God would be the crowning achievement of Jesus' life and ministry on the earth. It was what He was called to do, and He was very close to achieving it. And so, we find Jesus repeating this over and over in His prayer unto the Father: *"Father, I pray that they would be one just as We are one."*

If the truth of union with God was great, the truth it could take place on the earth was even greater. Notice Jesus did not pray for union to take place after we die and go to Heaven; Jesus pointed out that He was going to Heaven, but the disciples would be on the earth. Union with God would be for eternity, yet it would begin on the earth.

On the day of salvation, union with the Father begins! Even though you may be in this world, the more you consider yourself to be one with God, the easier it will be to disengage from the world's hold on you. It is from this position of union that we reign as kings in this life. Jesus summed up salvation by saying, *"That they would be one as We are one."* Friend, if you have received Jesus as your Savior, union with God is yours now.

If you have not received Jesus as your Savior, I ask you to do so now. Pray this with me:

> *God, I am a sinner, and I need a Savior. You said in Your Word, if I confess with my mouth the Lord Jesus and believe in my heart that You raised Jesus from the dead, I would be saved. God, I believe and confess Jesus to be my Lord!*

If you prayed that prayer, congratulations. You are a brand-new creature in Christ Jesus. You are righteous in God's sight and united with Him!

PRAYER

Father, thank You for loving me so much that You sent Jesus to unite us together. Jesus, thank You for the sacrifices You made on the earth so You could make the ultimate sacrifice and we could be one. Holy Spirit, open my eyes and help me to understand this union. I ask for greater revelation and insight into what salvation is truly all about. Jesus, reveal to me the greatness of this perfect union with You, the Father, and the Holy Spirit.

Chapter 4

"I KEPT THEM IN YOUR NAME"

While I was with them in the world, I kept them in Your name. Those whom You gave Me I have kept; and none of them is lost except the son of perdition, that the Scripture might be fulfilled (John 17:12).

When we read through the Gospels, we see that Jesus was hated by the religious people of the day. Jesus was not necessarily hated because of the miraculous works He did but for His message of union with God. Because of this, there were several murder attempts on

Jesus' life, and I would assume many attempts of physical assault as well. As we know, the more you do for God, the more satan is going to try and take you out.

We can't forget that through Jesus' journey, there was a great deal of danger. Not only was there the danger of people in the city trying to assault Jesus, there was also the danger of robbers on the outlying roads and wild animals in the countryside, as well as sickness and disease.

When Jesus called the disciples to Him, He didn't just call them to Him; Jesus called them *unto Him.* The disciples became the responsibility of Jesus; it was up to Jesus to provide for them financially as well as to protect them from all harm of physical and spiritual danger.

Jesus said, *"While I was with them in the world, I kept them in Your name."* Jesus lets us in on some wonderful truths regarding safety and protection while on the earth. First of all, we find out the reason none of the disciples were ever physically harmed or sick was because Jesus had taken ownership and responsibility for them. Secondly, we discover that the way Jesus did this was through operating according to His authority from Heaven.

It is important to understand that Jesus was under authority. He was a sinless man, anointed by God, filled with God, and sent by God into the earth with Heaven's authority. This authority far superseded the authority satan had on the earth before Jesus went to hell and took it from him.

> *Having disarmed principalities and powers, He made a public spectacle of them, triumphing over them in it* (Colossians 2:15).

When Jesus appeared to the disciples before He ascended to Heaven, Jesus said, *"All authority has been given to Me in heaven and on earth"* (Matt. 28:18). Jesus had only been operating in His heavenly authority, but it was all He needed to keep Himself and His own safe from all plagues and physical harm.

While Jesus was on the earth, He was operating in the name of God. We saw a tremendous example of this when the soldiers came to arrest Jesus in the garden of Gethsemane.

> *Jesus therefore, knowing all things that would come upon Him, went forward and said to them, "Whom are you seeking?" They answered Him, "Jesus of Nazareth." Jesus said to them, "I am He." And Judas, who betrayed Him, also stood with them. Now when He said to them, "I am He," they drew back and fell to the ground* (John 18:4–6).

In the Greek, Jesus literally said, "I AM." Jesus embodied not only God but His authority. Nothing could stand against Him. Jesus didn't act like most Christians and say, "Well, whatever will be will be. If something bad happens, it must have been God's will." No! Jesus didn't leave the safety of Himself and the disciples up to chance; Jesus intentionally used His authority and, with two words, knocked over six hundred soldiers on their backs. Jesus gave us an example of what was possible.

All the authority of Heaven was in God's name, but when Jesus arose victorious and our salvation was complete, the authority in the earth was added to that and then transferred to us! Therefore, Jesus said, *"All authority has been given to Me in Heaven and on earth. Go therefore and make disciples of all nations...."* (Matt. 28:18–19).

That's why Jesus told the disciples in John 14 that soon they would begin to use the name of Jesus. The authority would be transferred to Jesus, and because of our union with Him, we would have that authority as well.

We must realize Jesus was intentionally using His authority for safety and protection. Right before He went to the cross, there would be three days He would not be able to look after His disciples, and so Jesus asked the Father to protect them until Jesus could transfer that authority over to them. Once the authority was transferred, it would be the responsibility of us the Church to understand and skillfully and intentionally keep ourselves and those in our authority in His name.

We are living in the most dangerous days of the earth—constant wars, deadly diseases, weapons of mass destruction, and people filled with only evil. It's a dangerous time for the world and can even be a dangerous time for us Christians if we do not know the authority given to us.

Friend, we know we have authority in the name of Jesus, but we haven't even scratched the surface of what that means. If we did, we would boldly stand before any man and say,

> *I surrender my own life, and no one has the power to take my life from me. I have the authority to lay it down and the power to take it back again. This is the destiny my Father has set before me* (John 10:18 TPT).

We were not born of God and sent into the earth just for the earth to devour us. Remember, when God made Adam in His image and likeness, He gave man dominion over the earth. Adam lost it, but Jesus got it back and then gave it to us. Jesus is always our standard. He is the Way of Life, and if we live according to His example, nothing in this world can stop us.

Unfortunately, safety and protection are ours only as we choose to stay under submission to the

Lordship of Jesus and obey the leading of the Holy Spirit. Notice that when Jesus was praying, He said, *"Those whom You gave Me I have kept; and none of them is lost except the son of perdition."* Even though the disciples had been placed under the protection of Jesus, He could not protect those who would intentionally stray—and this is what happened with Judas. Jesus did not lose Judas; Judas lost himself.

Jesus has been given the responsibility of protecting and keeping us, but just as a mother hen cannot protect a chick that has wandered from the nest, neither can Jesus protect those who have walked away from Him.

Notice what the psalmist wrote in Psalm 91:

> *When you abide under the shadow of Shaddai, you are hidden in the strength of God Most High. He's the hope that holds me and the stronghold to shelter me, the only God for me, and my great confidence. He will rescue you from every hidden trap of the enemy, and he will protect you from*

false accusation and any deadly curse. His massive arms are wrapped around you, protecting you. You can run under his covering of majesty and hide. His arms of faithfulness are a shield keeping you from harm. You will never worry about an attack of demonic forces at night nor have to fear a spirit of darkness coming against you. Don't fear a thing! Whether by night or by day, demonic danger will not trouble you, nor will the powers of evil be launched against you. Even in a time of disaster, with thousands and thousands being killed, you will remain unscathed and unharmed (vv. 1–7 TPT).

God's promise was that as long as you stayed under the umbrella of His perfect will, you also remained under His protection; however, as powerful as God is, He will not usurp your free will. We all have a choice; we can choose well, or we can choose stupidly, and God will allow us to make our own choices. Now as a good and loving Father, He will show you what you need to do, but He will not make the choice for you.

This is where many Christians miss it. We make a stupid choice and then ask God to bless it. We disregard the leading of the Holy Spirit and then get mad at God because satan ran through the door we opened and used the authority we gave him.

Friend, do you realize we have it better than Psalm 91? Psalm 91 was the old covenant and was based on us abiding under His shadow; under the new covenant of grace, we are abiding IN HIM. We are in a position in Christ where we are impenetrable! To attack us is to attack Him!

As with Judas, the only way you can get lost is to lose yourself. Judas was with the group of Jesus but didn't see himself in the group. This is why it is so important to understand your true identity in Christ. If you don't know who you are in Him, you will lose your way. It doesn't matter how many Scriptures you know and how many church services you go to— demons know Scriptures and demons go to church too! Your safety is not about your intellect; it's about your identity and union with Christ. As we abide in Him and do what He tells us to do, He can protect us from the plans and attacks of satan. When you find yourself in Him, not only do your actions and behaviors change, but you put up a giant, three-hundred-and-sixty-degree, impenetrable wall of glory around yourself. Satan cannot touch the son or daughter of God who has found himself or herself in Christ.

PRAYER

Father, I thank You for Your protection over my life. Jesus, thank You for Your sacrifice to give me authority on this earth over the realm of death and every demonic force that may come my way. Father, I ask for greater revelation of the authority that exists in the name of Jesus. Open my eyes as to what is available, and help me to expand my soul as to what is possible. Holy Spirit, I ask You to teach me how to skillfully use the power and authority in this powerful name—the name above all names—not only for my protection, but also for those in my care. I declare today that in the name of Jesus, no sickness, no disease, no plague, and no danger shall come near my body or those who are under my care. I keep them in Your name!

Chapter 5

THE JOY OF JESUS

But now I come to You, and these things I speak in the world, that they may have My joy fulfilled in themselves (John 17:13).

There should never be such a thing as a depressed Christian; the Christian life is a joyful life! I understand there will be trials that come our way; there will be storms, and there will be giants, but when you know you already have the victory, it changes your response! Jesus said to be of good cheer because He had already conquered the world (see John 16:33)!

We may not be able to keep the birds from flying over our heads, but we can keep them from making a nest on our heads! Circumstances may come and go, but our joy is to remain the same because we can choose our response to those situations. We should never let the devil steal our joy by responding to life's negative situations with fear, anger, or depression!

Not only do we have a choice in the matter, but we also have the equipment from Heaven: We have the joy of the Lord! When Jesus was praying in the upper room, He said, *"These things I speak in the world, that they may have My joy fulfilled in themselves."* Have you ever thought about that? As Jesus was agonizing over what He was about to go through physically and spiritually, He was thinking about your joy. As He was going through a trial, Jesus was praying to the Father about your joy! And yet this wasn't just any joy—this was the joy of Jesus in you!

In John 15:11, Jesus said, *"These things I have spoken to you, that My joy may remain in you, and that your joy may be full."* In John 16:22, Jesus said, *"Therefore you now have sorrow; but I will see you again and your heart will rejoice, and your joy no one will take from you."* The joy of Jesus is a big deal! Jesus wants to see His joy fulfilled in you; for you to experience it, however, you must know you have it!

We have further proof of having joy in Galatians 5:

But the fruit of the Spirit is love, joy, peace, longsuffering, kindness, goodness, faithfulness, gentleness, self-control. Against such there is no law (vv. 22–23).

The contents of your recreated spirit united with God is His love, His peace, His patience, His goodness, His faithfulness, His gentleness, His self-control, and His joy! Jesus is the Vine, and you are the branch; what is flowing in Him is now flowing in you! These are not just fruits of the Holy Spirit; these are fruits of your recreated spirit in Christ. This is who you are! Friend, because of your union with Christ, all these wonderful traits are now part of you. You never have to have another sad day in your life!

I never could understand why people were always so sad at church; it was like people felt like, in order to be holy, they had to be sad. I went to a church as a kid where, as I told you in a previous chapter, every service ended with people at the altar crying. It was one thing if we were down at the altar praying or rejoicing, but they were always crying. I started listening to their "prayers," and the prayers were always about defeat. I didn't know much as a kid, but I knew something was wrong with the picture I saw each Sunday. In many cases, you couldn't tell if it was a church service or a funeral! Everyone looked depressed as they wiped tears away from their eyes.

I firmly believe the move of joy that flowed through the churches in the 1990s was of God. We had a lot of churches that were depressed because they didn't have any victory. We had another group of churches that understood some things about redemption but had so much teaching about God that they forgot they were also to experience God! In the 1990s, God was endeavoring to get His joy back in His Church! Why? Because the joy of the Lord is our strength! It's a powerful thing to be able to look right in the face of your enemy and laugh like God does!

*God laughs at the wicked and their plans,
for he knows their day is coming!* (Psalm
37:13 TPT).

God laughs at His enemies because He knows He
already has the victory! Do you realize that joy is a key
companion to your faith? There are a lot of defeated
Christians today simply because they lost their joy.
The circumstances of life came, and these Christians
allowed satan to steal their joy. But friend, you can't
be full of faith without being full of joy! Faith and joy
are best friends! Look at what the apostle Paul wrote
about this:

*Now may God, the fountain of hope, fill
you to overflowing with uncontainable joy
and perfect peace as you trust in him. And
may the power of the Holy Spirit continually surround your life with his super-abun-
dance until you radiate with hope!* (Romans
15:13 TPT).

Friend, you have the faith of Jesus, and coupled
with His faith, you have His peace and His joy! You

can believe for anything and stand before this cursed world in perfect peace and full of joy, knowing that peace and joy are yours.

Don't tell me you are in faith for something and yet you have a frown on your face and worry in your soul. I have had people sit in my office and tell me to my face that they are in faith for their healing, and yet I can see the worry all over their faces. Friend, there is no such thing as a person who is in faith and yet is depressed. You can't be in faith and depressed at the same time! Where you find faith, you will also find joy; they are inseparable!

If you are in faith for something, you will be at peace because you know it is all going to work out, and you will be full of joy because you know you have the victory in that situation. Believers are full of peace and full of joy—and I am not talking about something natural; I am talking about the peace and joy of Almighty God!

I think we forget that Jesus was a man of joy. If we were to have walked with Jesus during His earthly ministry, we would have seen a man not only who walked in the authority of Heaven, but also who walked in the joy of the Father. Jesus is a man who loves to have fun and laugh! I guarantee you the times between Jesus and the disciples were not all serious times; there were plenty of times of laughter and fun. I would dare say there was lots of laughter after all the miracles that took place. Can you imagine all the joy that was being experienced during the feeding of the four thousand and the five thousand? I guarantee there was lots of laughter among Jesus and the disciples! Why? Faith and joy are best friends, and there are always laughter and excitement when we see the manifestation of our faith.

I have found it interesting over the years that the Church has fallen into this state of thinking we have to be serious in order for God to move. There is this hidden and yet accepted belief that we must be really serious and somber for miracles to take place. The music has to be quiet, and we have to be quiet because God's business is serious business. It's almost as if you can't be holy and reverent without being really serious!

Friend, I'll let you in on a secret: God likes to have fun! God's business is serious business, but you don't always have to be serious to experience it. God is a God of joy! Certainly, there are the necessary times of worship and being still, but there are also the necessary times of rejoicing, shouting, and laughing. This is one reason I endeavor to keep things "light" in my healing services; I intentionally inject some humor into things and am always looking for opportunities to keep people from getting too serious. Now, if the Holy Spirit is leading things in a different direction, then I flow where He is going, but most of the time, our healing services are full of revelation, full of manifestations, and full of joy. God loves to laugh, and I'm telling you from firsthand experience, His laugh will rattle a room!

I'll never forget October 2005; I had an amazing experience in which I closed my eyes to go to sleep and found myself in Heaven. I won't go into all the details here, but the short version is I walked up a staircase and found myself in the throne room of God. When God saw me, He smiled, and I smiled back. Then He chuckled, and I chuckled. Then God laughed, and I laughed. Then God let out this big, boisterous laugh that literally shook the room like an earthquake had hit. The joy of the Father is amazing!

Well, what the Father has is what the Son has, and because of your union with Christ, you have it too. Jesus did not want you to simply have His joy, however; He wanted His joy fulfilled in you. In other words, Jesus wanted you to experience His joy in this life.

In this current time in the world, there are lots of things that could easily take your joy if you allowed them. If you allow your thoughts and emotions to get swept up by all the violence, wars, politics, economy, and host of other issues, you could get sad and angry very quickly—yet that is what satan wants. The moment you take a step out of the joy of the Lord, you step out of the faith of the Lord. If you want to be a person of strong faith, you must be a person of strong joy.

There are things Jesus needs to accomplish through you, and it is going to require your faith and your eyes to be fully on Him.

If you've lost your joy, you can get it back and go past the issue that was holding you back. No matter what situation you are going through right now, Jesus spoke those words so that your joy would be His joy. Even in the midst of pain and loss, you can still have joy. Certainly, we experience sadness in life, but it doesn't mean we must lose our joy. I know this is going to sound contradictory, but you can be sad and still have your joy. Sadness is an emotion; joy comes from Jesus. Sadness may come because of a loss, but Jesus is always there.

So, make the decision that in the sad times, you don't let the sadness turn into depression. Depression is not normal, and it is not of God. Depression is the result of an unchecked soul—allowing your thoughts and emotions to run wildly outside the boundaries of who you are in Christ. As spirit beings, we have control over our souls and our bodies. The joy of Jesus is a trait of our spirits, and for us to experience it, we must be spirit-ruled and spirit-conscious.

Galatians 5:23 tells us that one of the fruits of our recreated spirit is joy. It isn't something you need to obtain; it is part of your new identity in Christ. However, if you aren't knowledgeable that you are a spirit, you will look to the flesh to tell you how to feel. You must be conscious of who you are as a spirit and what you have as a spirit so you can experience the realities of who you have been made to be in Him. When you know His joy is yours, that you are a possessor of it, you can experience it whenever you want, wherever you want, regardless of the circumstances.

PRAYER

Jesus, thank You for Your joy! Holy Spirit, teach me how to walk in Your joy in a deeper and far greater level. Give me a greater revelation of this powerful reality! I ask for Your help in controlling my emotions and allowing Your joy and peace to flow through me and keep my emotions within the boundaries in which You intended. I pray that Your joy is fulfilled in me!

Chapter 6

"THE WORLD HAS HATED THEM"

*I have given them Your word; and
the world has hated them because
they are not of the world, just as I
am not of the world* (John 17:14).

We live in a world that is all about self; we live in
the age of the "selfie," where people's social media is
filled with images of themselves, and the goal is to get
as many "likes, hearts, and shares" as possible. We are
in a society that bases self-worth on how many followers we have; unfortunately, this has trickled into

the local church, where we base success on how many people are sitting in the chairs and watching online.

Whether you are in the ministry or the marketplace, you need to understand that Christianity is not a popularity contest, and the ministry was never meant to be an avenue to make you famous. There are too many in ministry today that have their sights on being Instagram famous instead of making Jesus famous. If fame comes as a result of ministry, then great, but it is not to be our motivating factor. In all reality, if the world loves you, it might not be the greatest compliment.

While praying in the upper room, Jesus said, *"The world has hated them because they are not of the world."* *Hate* is a strong word. According to Jesus, He and the disciples were not well liked or understood by those around them; of course, we do know that Jesus had several attempts on His life well before He went to the cross. Jesus wasn't hated because of the good works He did; He was hated because of the message He preached (see John 10:33).

Jesus preached that He was sent from Heaven to represent God His Father, and it did not go over well. Sure, Jesus had multitudes of people following Him, but how many were there following Him in the end? Many of the people who were in His church services for the miracles were the same ones who later yelled, "Crucify Him!"

As a Christian, if you are popular with the world, could it be because you are too much like the world? I know this is a hard-hitting question, but it must be asked of ourselves, especially in our current society. Certainly, we want to reach the world, but are we truly reaching the world if we are just like those in it? There has been such a move to tame our messages and be politically correct in order to be relevant that it seems the Church as a whole has become irrelevant.

When Jesus began to teach some "controversial" things, all His disciples left Him except for the original Twelve. As the others were leaving, Jesus looked at the Twelve and asked, "Are you going to leave too?" This wasn't Jesus begging; this was Jesus letting them know, "If you leave, I'm still moving forward."

This whole issue of the world hating disciples of Jesus (which includes you and me) goes far beyond our clothing or speech. Jesus' statement about the world hating us is about two things: identity and culture. According to William Barclay's commentary, in John's Gospel, "the world" stands for "human society organizing itself without God."[4]

Our identity is found in our union with Christ. We are Christ on the earth. We are the deliverers. We are the healers. We are the carriers of truth. We are the anointed ones in situations in which light needs to overcome darkness. Our culture is light. The world's culture is dark. We are the light of Heaven sent to shine in the world.

We are continual reminders of the difference between light and darkness. People of the darkness don't always like the light. Light exposes what is taking place in the darkness.

The beautiful message you've heard right from the start is that we should walk in self-sacrificing love toward one another.

We should not be like Cain, who yielded to the Evil One and brutally murdered his own brother, Abel. And why did he murder him? Because his own actions were evil and his brother's righteous. So don't be shocked, beloved brothers and sisters, if you experience the world's hatred (1 John 3:11–13 TPT).

The apostle who recorded Jesus' statement in the upper room is the same apostle who stated, *"So don't be shocked, beloved brothers and sisters, if you experience the world's hatred."* The apostle John knew something about the hatred of the world. In the book *Prescription Against Heretics*, Tertullian, a second-century North African theologian, stated:

Since, moreover, you are close upon Italy, you have Rome, from which there comes even into our own hands the very authority (of apostles themselves). How happy is its church, on which apostles poured forth all their doctrine along with their blood; where Peter endures a passion like his Lord's; where Paul wins his crown in a death like John [the Baptist's]; where the Apostle John was first plunged, unhurt, into boiling oil, and thence remitted to his island-exile.[5]

Church history tells us Roman Emperor Domitian commanded that John be boiled to death in oil, but John continued to preach from within the pot and could not be killed; as a result, John was exiled to Patmos, where he ended up writing the book of Revelation. The youngest of the disciples ended up being the one to live the longest and yet experienced continued persecution from a world that hated him. Why? Because John not only had a revelation of the life of God and that life not only protected him, but also exposed the darkness in other people's lives. In a world that is increasingly becoming dark, don't expect to be well liked when you shine the light.

There is a reason that we are seeing increased opposition and persecution of Christianity in the

United States. In the rest of the world, such opposition has been common for a very long time, but as the Church has gravitated more toward becoming seeker sensitive, the Church has in reality become blind to the dark. We have found the Church more and more accepting of what the world calls normal. We are seeing more groups accepting abortion and all forms of sexual immorality; as a result, we have seen more ministers fall prey to immorality than at any time before.

As the Church began to dim its light so as not to offend, the darkness grew darker—not only in the world, but also in the Church! As a result, the Church has lost the little influence she used to have in society. It's impossible to shine your light brightly when you intentionally make it dim. We were made to stand out—not blend in!

It is time the Church heads toward the light and begins to take her place as the salt and light from Heaven. Light not only exposes, but it disinfects and cleanses! It is time that we begin to stand up and declare to the world that Jesus is the Way, the Truth, and the Life. Don't get offended when you declare Jesus is the Healer while the world scoffs at you because you don't trust their science!

I have taken a lot of flack from the world for my stance on healing and, unfortunately, from Christians as well. During the Covid pandemic, Lacy and I were still pastoring. While almost everyone closed their church doors in our city, we adamantly refused. Someone had to be a light in our community, and I was determined it would be us. I couldn't preach healing and yet shut my church down because of a disease; I would have been a hypocrite. Why would I declare Jesus is the Healer but not when there was a pandemic?

Most of the people in our church supported my stance, but I was shocked at the vile hatred I received from most of the community. Lacy didn't know it at the time, but I started getting death threats. The local news did a story on us, and it went viral. Why did it go viral? Because when asked why I wasn't afraid of the virus, I quoted 2 Corinthians 5:21 and said, "Jesus died with my sins and with Covid so that I didn't have to." The story was picked up by *Newsweek* and eventually the Associated Press. Within a few days, we were in almost every newspaper across the country, and I was getting emails from CNN and other news outlets asking for more stories—which I refused to provide. We were getting emails and phone calls from angry people all around the world letting us know that they hoped we all died horrible deaths because we didn't believe the science. The governor of Arkansas was talking about us in his daily press conferences and was threatening to shut us down.

So why was all this happening? It wasn't because we were being unsafe; we were following all the requested guidelines of social distancing, sanitization, and occupancy. All the demonic hatred was because my light was exposing the darkness all around us, and the demons operating in these people didn't like it.

> *And here is the basis for their judgment: The Light of God has now come into the world, but the people loved darkness more than the Light, because they want the darkness*

> *to conceal their evil. So the wicked hate the*
> *Light and try to hide from it, for the Light*
> *fully exposes their lives. But those who love*
> *the truth will come into the Light, for the*
> *Light will reveal that it was God who*
> *produced their fruitful works* (John 3:19–
> 21 TPT).

All the evil in this world has satan behind it. All those who aren't saved are ignorantly led by him in their actions and emotions, and unfortunately, all the carnal Christians who are more curse-conscious than God-conscious are led by satan too. When you begin to walk in the light, don't be surprised when much of the world hates you for it. But when you walk in your union with Christ, the only possible result is the manifestation of light. Why? Because Jesus is the Light of Life!

> *A fountain of life was in him, for his life is*
> *light for all humanity. And this Light never*
> *fails to shine through darkness—Light that*
> *darkness could not overcome!* (John 1:4–5
> TPT).

The life of God produces light, and this life was in Christ and was the same life Jesus came to give you and me. When we walk in our union with Him, we walk in the life that produces light—light that will heal disease, expose darkness, and destroy the results of the curse. The darkness and the sons of darkness cannot overpower that life!

We used to sing a song in church when I was a child called "This Little Light of Mine." Just like religion does, it was a song of truth sprinkled with poison. The lyrics said:

> *This little light of mine*
> *I'm going to let it shine*
> *Let it shine, all the time, let it shine*
> *Hide it under a bushel? No!*
> *I'm going to let it shine*
> *Let it shine, all the time, let it shine.*
> *Don't let satan blow it out!*
> *I'm going to let it shine*
> *Let it shine, all the time, let it shine*

Friend, I have a light to shine, but it isn't little! It is so big it can't be hidden under a bushel, which is the equivalent of a five-gallon bucket! How we have sold our salvation short! I have the light of Almighty God in my spirit, and satan can't blow it out; he can't even touch it without that light knocking him out! The light that was released into the universe in Genesis 1 is what is inside you and me through our union with Christ (see 2 Cor. 4:6).

Friend, Jesus is THE WAY—no matter what the circumstances may be. It is a narrow road, not a popular road, that we walk. Jesus never promised the glory life would be a popular life. Unfortunately, too many today are in the ministry, seeking fame and fortune. In this life, it is not about how many followers and subscribers you have; it is about how much light you shine.

Be bold about this wonderful gospel message of union with the Father. If that simple message brought persecution to Jesus, it will bring persecution to you; no servant is above His master (see John 15:20). For people to be saved, filled, healed, and delivered, the light of Jesus must be shined—and yet, it is impossible in shining the light that it will not bring about persecution from those who love the darkness. You are an alien in this world and were meant to stick out because of the glory that permeates the world through you.

Choose to be bold in your speech, and yet let it be seasoned with grace; at the same time, refuse to be offended but be motivated by love. Shine the light and manifest His Kingdom for all the world to see.

PRAYER

Father, I ask You to help me walk in the love that Jesus walked in. I desire to walk in great boldness of speech and reveal Jesus as the Way, the Truth, and the Life. Help me to grow in my revelation of all that I am in You and all that You are in me; I want my light to shine brighter and brighter. May the light in me expose the darkness in the world and bring many unto You.

Chapter 7

"KEEP THEM FROM THE EVIL ONE"

*I do not pray that You should take them
out of the world, but that You should keep
them from the evil one* (John 17:15).

In some ways, we have misrepresented the true focus of salvation. We ask people, "If you died today, would you go to Heaven or hell?" It's interesting, though, that Jesus never made the focus of salvation about going to Heaven. As we discussed in chapter three, the purpose of salvation wasn't to change your destination, but to change your position. The purpose of salvation wasn't primarily to take you somewhere, but to get Someone in you!

Jesus didn't come to take you to Heaven; Jesus came to unite you with God! Now certainly, there is a very real Heaven and a very real hell, and salvation does provide a one-way ticket to Heaven. However, going to Heaven was not the focus of salvation; it is one of the byproducts.

One of the byproducts of salvation is that when you take your last breath, you get to go to Heaven. If the entire focus of salvation was on you going to Heaven, then the moment you said, "Jesus, I receive You as my Lord and Savior," then you would have immediately gone out of here!

There is a reason that you do not immediately go to Heaven; it is because not only does God need you to do some growing up in the things of God, but He also needs you to represent Him on the earth as a true son or daughter of God. Jesus needs you to make Him known to a world that does not know Him. Jesus needs you in the world.

Friend, this is where the Church missed it many years ago; we thought holiness was about being separated physically from the world—but that was totally wrong! Jesus needs us in the world so He can manifest His light for the world. How can we help a world that we exclude ourselves from? You can be in the world and yet not of it; you can be in the world and yet not be influenced by it. But how can you influence a world you have isolated yourself from? Jesus did not isolate Himself from the sinner; Jesus walked among them, ate with them, and fellowshipped with them because He believed what was in Him was far greater than what was in them.

While Jesus was praying in the upper room, He said, *"Father, I do not pray that You take them out of the world but that You keep them from the evil one."* Notice Jesus was not trying to get us out of the earth immediately upon salvation. Why? Because we have a job to do! Jesus was about to die and be in hell for three days; He wasn't going to be around to help guard and protect the disciples from the attacks of satan during that time. As a result, Jesus was praying beforehand and putting His request in the hands of God:

"Protect, keep, and guard the ones You gave Me from the attacks of satan."

However, despite Jesus wanting us to stay here for a while, Jesus did recognize there was an enemy in this world, and that enemy is satan. Jesus said, *"I pray that You keep them from the evil one."* The word *keep* in the Greek means to "attend to carefully, to take care of or to guard."[6]

It is interesting that in some religious circles, people actually deny the existence of hell and satan—even though Jesus acknowledged hell and satan as being very real. During Jesus' time on the earth, He had many satanic attacks come against Him. Not only was Jesus tempted by satan for forty days in the wilderness, but satan also stirred up the religious people to try and kill Jesus numerous times.

In addition to the attacks on Jesus, there were also schemes and attacks against the disciples. As Jesus and the disciples partook of the Passover meal in the upper room, satan came against Judas and used him to carry out the plan against Jesus.

At that time Satan himself entered into Judas the locksmith, who was one of the twelve apostles. He secretly went to the religious hierarchy and the captains of the temple guards to discuss with them how he could betray Jesus and turn him over to their hands (Luke 22:3–4 TPT).

Notice this was not one of satan's minions; satan took on this task himself to make sure the job got done. There was a reason satan was able to use Judas; it was because Judas' heart was impure. God cannot keep those who do not want to be kept. Judas had continued to have an unmaintained thought life and eventually gave into the temptations and deceptions of satan. Not too long after satan used Judas as his pawn, we find out that satan was also trying to find a way to use Peter as well.

While Jesus and the disciples were eating the Passover meal, Jesus warned Peter about satan:

Simon, Simon! Indeed, Satan has asked for you, that he may sift you as wheat. But I have prayed for you, that your faith should not fail; and when you have returned to Me, strengthen your brethren (Luke 22:31–32).

Just as with the story of Job in the Old Testament, we find that satan was petitioning God for the downfall of certain disciples of Jesus. Unfortunately, Job had no one to pray for him. Peter and Judas had Jesus in their corner to pray for them, but even Jesus had limits to His prayer because of free will and justice. There was a separating factor between Judas and Peter. They were both disciples of Jesus and had been with Jesus over three years; the difference was their hearts.

Peter's heart was right before Jesus. Yes, Peter said and did some ignorant things, but his heart and motivation were always pure toward Jesus. Because his heart was right, it put Jesus in a position to be able to pray for Peter and get results. On the other hand, Judas' heart was not right, and it put him in a position to be used by satan. As the treasurer, Judas had access to the ministry money and would steal money whenever he wanted to (see John 12:6). This continued, and unchecked sin led to open doors for satan into Judas' life until, eventually, Judas betrayed Jesus and then Judas committed suicide. This simply goes to show that satan is always looking for inroads into your life. He will find the weak spot in your life, and if you do not strengthen that area, satan will continue to widen it and gain more control over your life to use you as his pawn; then, when satan is done with you, he will simply dispose of you.

Friend, there is an enemy in this world that is looking to destroy you. The good news is, because of our union with Christ, we already have the victory over satan; it is now our responsibility to enforce that victory. When Jesus paid the price for our justification, God raised Him up, and then Jesus stripped satan of his authority over us. However, just because satan has been defeated, it hasn't stopped him from looking for those he can devour. As 1 Peter 5:8 instructs us, *"Be well balanced and always alert, because your enemy, the devil, roams around incessantly, like a roaring lion looking for its prey to devour"* (TPT).

Notice satan roams incessantly, looking for someone to devour. During one of my trips to Kenya, I spent time interviewing some former witch doctors, one of whom is now a pastor. In talking about satan's operations in the world, the former witch doctor said, "Satan works around the clock to try and keep the will of God from working. He knows who are the Christians but also knows what their weaknesses are." He went on to say, "As a witch doctor, when I saw a Christian who knew who they were, I would feel their power hitting all over my body, and I would have to leave."

Satan cannot devour anyone he wants; he can only devour the one who refuses to maintain their thought life or does not know who they are as a true son or daughter of God. This is why we are told to stay alert. Every temptation that comes your way is simply satan looking for an inroad into your life. The devil's purpose is to continually make you less conscious of God to the point that the devil can destroy you. Our responsibility is to be alert, and when satan shows up with his lies, temptations, and deceptions, we resist him.

I am so thankful we not only have authority over satan, but we have Jesus looking out for us! Jesus took on the responsibility of prayer for His disciples back then, and He is still taking on the responsibility of prayer today! Jesus, as our High Priest, is our Intercessor!

> *Who then is left to condemn us? Certainly not Jesus, the Anointed One! For he gave his life for us, and even more than that he has conquered death and is now risen, exalted, and enthroned by God at his right hand. So how could He possibly condemn us since he is continually praying for our triumph?* (Romans 8:34 TPT)

Just as Jesus was praying for the disciples' protection and triumph, Jesus is doing the same for you and me! Glory to God! Friend, there will be tests and trials that come our way. The more we progress in our understanding of our union with Christ, the more we will be a threat to satan's defeated kingdom on this earth. As a result of our continued growth, there will be giants, mountains, and storms—but I have good news! Even though there will be giants to slay, mountains to move, and storms to still, Jesus has already prayed for your triumph! Jesus is praying for your protection! Jesus is praying for your strength! Jesus is praying, my friend! As long as we come into agreement with His prayers by believing them with our hearts, confessing them with our mouths, and walking out what the Holy Spirit is leading us to do, we will always triumph, and satan will not be able to stop it!

Prayer

Jesus, thank You for the victory You have provided for me. I thank You that You have conquered the world and its systems. You see the future and what is ahead of me. Thank You for praying for my safety, protection, and deliverance. Holy Spirit, I ask You to help me increase my sensitivity to Your voice so that I hear more clearly as to what to say and do. Jesus, reveal to me Your prayers for me so that I could come more closely in alignment with them. While I am here on the earth, I will fulfill all You have called me to do. No matter what trial that comes my way, I will enter it in faith, with joy and peace in my soul, knowing You have already prayed out my victory!

Chapter 8

"NOT OF THE WORLD"

They are not of the world, just as I am not of the world (John 17:16).

Your identity is largely comprised of your place of origin, citizenship, race, and ethnicity. Where you are from, the culture you are born into, the language of that culture, and the customs of that place play a tremendous role in shaping who you are. Where you are from has such a huge impact on your identity that it also plays a role in determining your self-esteem, habits, life goals, etc. In many ways, we are products of our own environment.

Jesus revealed a massive piece of His identity and our identity when He said in the upper room, *"They are not of the world, just as I am not of the world."* This reality was so important to Jesus that in the book of John, Jesus actually referred to being from Heaven forty-one times! What is even more interesting is that the book of John only represents approximately nineteen days of Jesus' earthly ministry. So, in nineteen days, Jesus mentioned that He is from Heaven forty-one times!

Most of us have a pretty firm understanding that Jesus was from Heaven; yet again, the key is that *Jesus understood He was from Heaven.* We often forget Jesus was doing life as a man anointed by God (see Acts 10:38). Jesus had humbled Himself, laid aside everything that gave Him an advantage, and came to the earth as a man (see Phil. 2:6–7). Jesus had to learn who He was just like we have to, and He had to renew His mind to the realities of who He truly was in the same way we do. One of the staggering realities Jesus had to grasp and accept was His origin—and He accepted it in a tremendous way. Jesus knew Heaven was His home:

> *No one has ever gone up to heaven, but there is One who has come down from heaven—the Son of Man [Himself—whose home is in heaven]* (John 3:13 AMP).

> *Jesus answered and said to them, "Even if I bear witness of Myself, My witness is true, for I know where I came from and where I am going; but you do not know where I come from and where I am going." . . . And He said to them, "You are from beneath; I am from above. You are of this world; I am not of this world"* (John 8:14, 23).

Jesus plainly stated to the religious people of the day that Earth was not His home. I love the boldness in which Jesus spoke the truth. He essentially told the Pharisees in John 8, "You are from hell; I am from Heaven." Can you imagine telling someone that? Yet, this is what Jesus said.

We must understand why it was so important that Jesus understood where He was from. Jesus' understanding His origin was crucial because, if He didn't, it would have hindered Him in fulfilling God's plan for His life. Remember, forty-one times Jesus referred to His heavenly origin. This was an extremely important truth for Him; therefore, it is an extremely important truth for you and me.

You may be saying, "Well, that's fine and all. I know that Jesus was from Heaven, and I understand that Jesus knew He was from Heaven—but what does this mean for me?" Well, did you see what Jesus said?

> *They are not of the world, just as I am not of the world* (John 17:16).

Just like Jesus, as a believer, you are not of this world. There are two important words in that scripture that really stand out to me: *just as. Merriam-Webster Dictionary* defines the phrase *just as* to mean "to an equal degree; in the same way as." In the very same way Jesus is not from here, you are not from here.

Why? Because when you have been born again; you were born from Heaven.

> *Jesus answered him, "I assure you and most solemnly say to you, unless a person is born again [reborn from above—spiritually transformed, renewed, sanctified], he cannot [ever] see and experience the kingdom of God"* (John 3:3 AMP).
>
> *If you were of the world, the world would love its own. Yet because you are not of the world, but I chose you out of the world, therefore the world hates you* (John 15:19).

Again, this is Jesus talking. Did you see what He said about you? Here is more proof from the mouth of Jesus Christ that you are not from here. What you experience with your five senses is not your home and not your place of origin. You may have been born on the earth, but you were born from Heaven. When you accepted Jesus Christ as your Lord and Savior, you became a brand-new creature; you became a being filled with God. The old you passed away, and a brand-new you was born (see 2 Cor. 5:17)! When you received salvation, you became brand-new with a new identity and a new origin.

You have to understand that you are a spirit being; the real you is not what you see in the mirror—that is just your physical house for your spirit. The Bible plainly tells us that we are three-part beings (see 1 Thess. 5:23). You are a spirit, you have a soul (your mind, will, and emotions), and you have a body. When you accepted salvation, your spirit became brand-new, yet the mind you think with and the body you walk with stay the same. For this reason, the apostle Paul made statements like "renew your mind" and "crucify your flesh," because those two things weren't saved; they were not made new like your spirit was.

Just like with your natural citizenship, your spiritual citizenship occurs the same way: by birth. If you were born in the United States, then you automatically became or were a citizen of the United States. When you were born again, you automatically became or were a citizen of Heaven. Citizenship is by birth. If someone's citizenship is in hell, then there is good news: They can change citizenship by being born again! The doors of heavenly citizenship are always open, and the stamp of the blood of Jesus forever seals that citizenship.

> *For our citizenship is in heaven, from which we eagerly await for the Savior, the Lord Jesus Christ* (Philippians 3:20).

You may have been born in the United States, France, Mexico, Australia, India, or some other country, but it's not the origin of the true you. You are from another world with a temporary existence on this planet called Earth.

Saved or unsaved, we are spirit beings with a spiritual origin. If you have never accepted salvation, then your home is hell. Some people may not like that but it's not my opinion—it is Bible! If you have accepted salvation, then Heaven is your home and your place of citizenship.

Like Jesus, you have Heaven as your home. It was extremely important for this to be a reality in His life, and it's extremely important for it to be a reality in your life. Say it with me, "Heaven is my home! It's where I am from and where I am going!"

Even those in the Old Testament like King David and Abraham had an understanding about this truth; they understood their time here on the earth was just temporary. They understood they were aliens in this world and Heaven was to be their actual home.

> *For we are aliens and pilgrims before You, as were all our fathers; our days on earth are as a shadow, and without hope* (1 Chronicles 29:15).

> *All these died in faith [guided and sustained by it], without receiving the [tangible fulfillment of God's] promises, only having seen (anticipated) them and having greeted them from a distance, and having acknowledged that they were strangers and exiles on the earth* (Hebrews 11:13 AMP).

The difference between the Old Testament saints and you is that they were waiting for Heaven to be their home; because of our union with Christ, Heaven is already our home!

If you ever wondered if aliens are real, then look in the mirror, and you'll discover that they are! You are an alien from another world: Heaven. When we get a revelation of this marvelous truth, it will change our lives. Heaven is where you and I are from!

"I am a supernatural being with a supernatural origin living in a natural world." This must be your mindset. It must be how you view yourself; otherwise, regardless of your heavenly origin, you will succumb to and be complacent in living a very natural, ordinary life subject to the circumstances around you.

You are in the world, but you are not of this world. You are from another planet. You are a different breed of being, a different species of life on planet Earth. Your citizenship is in Heaven, and you received it by birth!

PRAYER

Jesus, thank You for giving Your life so I could be born again and birthed from Heaven. Holy Spirit, give me a greater revelation of my origin. Help me to renew my mind to where I am from so I can manifest Heaven to a greater degree. I declare that Heaven is my home! Heaven is my culture! Heaven is my normal!

Chapter 9

AN ALTERNATE REALITY

Sanctify them by Your truth.
Your word is truth (John 17:17).

We have just seen where Jesus stated He was not of this world and we are not of this world. Jesus was, in all respects, an alien; He was born in Heaven, sent from Heaven, and sent into this earth to do a job and then return to Heaven. Being sent from another world was very much in the consciousness of Jesus.

Jesus continued in His prayer in John 17:17 and said, *"Sanctify them by Your truth. Your word is truth."*

In this short statement lies a hidden yet powerful revelation for us around which Jesus' entire prayer is wrapped. The word *sanctify* is the Greek word *hagiazo* which means "to consecrate, separate or purify."[7] So, Jesus' prayer is for the Father to separate them by His truth. Now, this is where things get interesting. Most people would read over this and simply take this statement that when we live by the words of God, it will help us to live separate and pure lives that will distinguish us from the sinner. Although it is true that living according to God's commands will help us live holy lives, this statement Jesus made was not about that—it was way more than that!

The word *truth* here is the Greek word *aletheia* and can simply be defined as *reality*. Essentially, Jesus said, "Father, separate them from the world by Your reality. Your Word is reality." Now, look at this closely. Jesus was talking about another reality here, an alternate reality—*something different than what everyone else is experiencing.*

Jesus gave us a major clue as to why He was getting supernatural results. How was He walking on water, calming storms, turning water into wine, multiplying food, raising the dead, and healing the sick? Jesus was living life as a man, anointed by God but living according to another reality. He wasn't living according to the reality of this world with its impossibilities; Jesus was living in an alternate reality while on the earth, and it was His desire that the disciples (which include you and me) would live permanently in this alternate reality as well.

Jesus' time with the disciples was not to simply make them good, moral, well-behaved men. Jesus' time with the disciples was to make them representatives of Heaven with power and authority exactly as Jesus had while on the earth. It was Jesus' desire and purpose for the disciples to replicate Him with perfection so that even when Jesus was no longer on the earth, the same ministry of power would continue through all those who became united with Him through salvation.

So, what is this alternate reality? It is a reality of the blessing which God gave to Adam in the garden of Eden.

> *So God created man in His own image; in the image of God He created him; male and female He created them. Then God blessed them, and God said to them, "Be fruitful and multiply; fill the earth and subdue it; have dominion over the fish of the sea, over the birds of the air, and over every living thing that moves on the earth"* (Genesis 1:27–28).

Before Adam sinned, Adam had complete dominion over the earth and everything in it; there was nothing that was not under his control. He not only had control over the animals, Adam had control over the earth. The water, the ground—all of it was under Adam's authority. Look at what people like Moses, Joshua, Elijah, Elisha, and Jesus did with nature; if they could accomplish that AFTER the curse, imagine what Adam was able to do BEFORE the curse!

Adam was living in the blessing. The Kingdom of God was in complete dominion. There was no sickness, no death, and no lack, and Adam and Eve had unhindered access to Heaven because there was no sin. However, the moment Adam sinned, EVERY-THING changed; his reality changed. His physical senses began to slowly become the leader of his life, and his spiritual sensitivity began to slowly fade away.

There was then a new reality for Adam, a reality dominated by the curse: a life that would be ruled by death. Adam went from being a guardian to a gardener. His sole job in the garden of Eden was to guard and protect what was provided to him; then Adam would have to work for everything he needed. Adam traded a weapon for a shovel and went from being a watchman to a worker. In the garden, everything Adam needed for life was already provided. It was a life of grace, and he traded it for a life of works in a reality ruled by the curse.

All living things began to decay. The life of God that was in mankind to protect it from all sickness, disease, pain, and decay was gone. Man was left to his own understanding and ways, walking according to the world of death. Access to Heaven was shut. Sickness and disease would reign supreme. Flu season and allergy season would become just as normal as winter, spring, summer, and fall. Doctors would eventually take the place of God as the source of healing, and the love of many began to grow cold. This is what became the reality of the world: a life of limitations, death, destruction, famine, poverty, disease, and dependence on self.

The world's reality is what is normal for us because it is what we have grown up in. From the time you arrived in this world, you became indoctrinated by society that getting a cold is normal. If you get a fever or sore throat during the winter season, it is normal. If you get a headache or muscle aches, the solution is to take some aspirin or other over-the-counter medications. The world's reality tells us that if someone is diagnosed with cancer, the only "real" solution is for them to undergo chemotherapy and/or radiation. This reality looks at doctors as the sole source of physical help. You are told all these things as you grow up. Your family, teachers, church, media, and society tell you all these things are a normal part of life. Sickness, lack, impossibilities—they are everywhere you go! It is the world's reality.

As a result, what used to be normal in the garden of Eden became things available only by living a life of faith for those who would pursue them, and yet those who did were few and far between. The reality of Heaven would become an alternate reality, and the reality of a curse-filled and dominated world became the reality of humanity.

Throughout the thousands of years before Jesus' first coming, there were a few that caught a glimpse of this alternate reality, and for brief moments, they accessed it and manifested Heaven. They raised the dead, divided waters, healed the sick, stopped the sun—the stories of some of the Old Testament saints sometimes read like a superhero story. Some would say it was because they were special; no, it was because they lived according to this alternate reality. It may have been for days at a time or only for a few minutes, but every time they did, the supernatural became natural, and the impossible became possible in that moment.

> *Dear, dear Corinthians, I can't tell you how much I long for you to enter this wide-open,*

spacious life. We didn't fence you in. The smallness you feel comes from within you. Your lives aren't small, but you're living them in a small way. I'm speaking as plainly as I can and with great affection. Open up your lives. Live openly and expansively! (2 Corinthians 6:11–13 MSG).

The cry of God for His creation is to live this wide open, spacious life, free of the limitations of this cursed reality. There is a reason that innately, we identify with superheroes and constantly look for ways to go beyond the limitations we experience with our senses. Instinctively, we know there should be more but can't see it because of the dullness of our hearts.

While others are living according to the world's reality of death and decay, we can live in the world's reality and yet live according to an alternate reality, a reality that supersedes that which most of humanity knows—the ability to look at death and yet see life; to look at a mountain and see it as a molehill; to look at a live cancer and yet see it as dead. It was this alternate reality that Jesus came not only to introduce, but also make possible for us to live in, live from, and manifest while alive on the earth.

There are many scriptural reasons we see as to why Jesus came to the earth. Yes, we know Jesus came to save us, but He also came to do several other things: one of them being to show us what was possible as a man or woman filled and united with God. Jesus was not only revealing the Father, but He was also revealing what was possible when we see and think like the Father.

In John 14:6, Jesus made a statement that is very familiar but has been glossed over. He said, *"I am the way, the truth, and the life."* We understand Jesus is the only way to the Father; as much as that is coming under attack in our current society, there is no other way to the Father but by Jesus! After declaring that He is the way, He declares that He is the truth. But remember, this word *truth* means reality! In other words, not only were the words and actions of Jesus the truth, but they were also reality. Jesus was revealing an alternate reality.

Jesus' ministry was not just bringing salvation and revealing the love of the Father, but it was also combatting the impossibilities of the physical realm and showing another world from which to live. Jesus was endeavoring to show His disciples how to live as a son of blessing as opposed to a son of the curse. For this reason, when Jesus sent the disciples out to preach and heal the sick, it was to be a manifestation of the Kingdom of God, the alternate realities of Heaven usurping the realities of the cursed world.

> *Whatever city you enter, and they receive you, eat such things as are set before you. And heal the sick there, and say to them, "The kingdom of God has come near to you." But whatever city you enter, and they do not receive you, go out into its streets and say, "The very dust of your city which clings to us we wipe off against you. Nevertheless know this, that the kingdom of God has come near you"* (Luke 10:8–11).

Notice that the sick being healed was an experience of the Kingdom of God, the righteousness of

God overriding the unrighteousness of the world. It was the experience of an alternate reality, a reality greater than what we experience with our physical senses. For those who refused to receive the message of the Kingdom of God, they were told the opportunity had been there to experience it, but because by choice, they had missed it. An alternate reality was available, but by their very own choosing, they continued to live according to this world's reality.

If you want to see Heaven's reality, simply look at Jesus. Jesus showed us what the will of God was on the earth. Jesus showed us what was possible as a man or woman filled with God and united with God. I am thankful for the powerful men and women of God who have come before us as examples to follow; however, Jesus is my standard. It is Jesus by whom I will always measure everything and determine what should be in my life and how I should handle it.

Jesus showed us what was possible as a man living on the Earth but living from Heaven; if we are to do the works of Jesus, however, we must share the same perspective He had while on the earth.

PRAYER

Father, I desire to walk according to the reality Jesus showed was available on the earth. Holy Spirit, I ask You for revelation on this alternate reality. I pray for greater insight and understanding into the ways of Heaven and how to manifest the will of Heaven on this earth. Father, it is my desire that my words and actions be a living example of Jesus in action. Help me to see myself according to Your reality so that I show myself as separate from the world. May my life be an overflow of Heaven, bringing You glory on the earth.

Chapter 10

SENT INTO THE WORLD

As You sent Me into the world, I also have sent them into the world (John 17:18).

We have seen thus far that Heaven is our home; it is not a religious statement but a spiritual fact. When we are born again, we are born from above. In Jesus' prayer, Jesus not only stated this fact, but then He went on to say, *"As You sent Me into the world, I also have sent them into the world."*

This statement carries some serious revelation about our identity, our purpose, and our ability. First, notice the word *sent*; to be sent into a place, you must come from another place. That is not rocket science; it is just common sense! I can't go into a place where I already am.

Jesus said, *"You sent Me into the world."* Well, this must mean Jesus came from somewhere else, and we have already seen this to be true. Jesus came from Heaven. Over and over throughout the book of John, Jesus talked about being sent from Heaven.

> *Jesus said to them, "My food is to do the will of Him who sent Me, and to finish His work"* (John 4:34).

> *For I have come down from heaven, not to do My own will, but the will of Him who sent Me* (John 6:38).

> *Jesus answered them and said, "My doctrine is not Mine, but His who sent Me"* (John 7:16).

> *But I know Him, for I am from Him, and He sent Me* (John 7:29).

*And He who sent Me is with Me. The Father
has not left Me alone, for I always do those
things that please Him* (John 8:29).

Being a sent one was a big deal to Jesus; if He
was talking about it a lot, it is because He was thinking about it even more! Well, Jesus did not just stop
with that statement about Himself—He went on to
include us! *"As You sent Me into the world, I also have
sent them into the world."* In the very same way God
sent Jesus, Jesus has sent us.

The word *sent* is the Greek word *apostello*. As you
can probably guess, it's where we get the English word
apostle. An apostle is a sent one. In a very general sense,
all of us have an apostolic call because we have all been
sent by Jesus into the world. Certainly, there are those
in the apostolic office who have been sent by Jesus as
an apostle to a country or for a certain work, but again,
in a general sense, we are all sent ones. We are ambassadors for Christ. We have all been given the ministry
of representing Jesus and endeavoring to bring people
into relationship with God (see 2 Cor. 5:20). Because

of this, we are all important. Just because you may not be standing behind a pulpit or leading a large ministry does not mean you are less important.

In Jesus' prayer, we discover not only our identity as sent ones, but we also discover our purpose. What is our purpose? Look at Jesus! What was Jesus doing on the earth? He was manifesting Heaven on the earth and destroying the works of darkness!

> *For this purpose the Son of God was manifested, that He might destroy the works of the devil* (1 John 3:8).

Just as the Father sent Jesus into the world to manifest the Kingdom of God, Jesus sent you and me to continue manifesting the Kingdom of God. Jesus was undoing the works of satan in people's lives. Friend, just as the Father sent Jesus, Jesus sent us—don't ever forget that! The only thing Jesus was sent to do that we could never do was die as the Redeemer of the world—that alone was reserved for Jesus Christ; however, the works Jesus did on the earth, we were sent to do as well. We have been given the responsibility of being ambassadors of Heaven! We are the light in this world! We have the privilege to stand on Jesus' behalf before the works of darkness and command them to cease. When we walk into a place of unrighteousness, because of our righteousness in Him, we stand in the position to right the wrong.

As sent ones from Heaven, we are not to conform; we are to transform. There are too many Christians today trying to fit in with the world; however, Jesus sent us to stand out! Remember, we are to be set apart by His reality. We are to get different results than the rest of the world. When the world is getting sick, we are to remain healthy. When the world is going broke, we are to be prospering. When the world is in fear, we are to be at peace. Why? Because we were sent into this world to live from another reality so we can manifest that reality on the earth.

We are to stand out because of the glory of God in our lives. The light that shines in us should be shining through our family, our finances, our health, our businesses, and yes, even our ministries. We are to stand out not only because of our identity and purpose as sent ones, but also because we have the resources to fulfill the plan of God for our lives on the earth.

Isn't it interesting you never saw Jesus in Scripture asking God for more power? God sent Jesus fully supplied! When Jesus stood before a sickness or disease, Jesus never had to question if He had enough authority and power to get the job done; Jesus had more than enough! It would have been unjust for God to send Jesus into the world to destroy the works of darkness and yet not give Jesus the spiritual equipment He needed. Jesus never said the things the modern Church says. The modern Church is singing and praying, "God pour out Your Spirit. Pour out Your power. We need more!" Isn't it funny that Jesus never did that? So why are we asking for things Jesus didn't ask for? Could it be that we do not fully understand our union with Christ?

We must remember what the apostle John wrote about Jesus:

> *And from the overflow of his fullness we received grace heaped upon more grace!* (John 1:16 TPT).

Do you see this? From His fullness we received grace heaped upon more grace! That does not sound like we are lacking—in any way! God never gives just a little bit; God is an excessive, lavish, and abundant Giver. God always gives too much!

Heaps of grace—this is what we have in order to represent Jesus. Grace for our health! Grace for our relationships! Grace for our finances!

Not only did God send Jesus into the world spiritually supplied, God also sent Jesus physically supplied. Isn't it interesting you never saw Jesus asking God for money? We never see Jesus lacking financially during His earthly ministry. Now, I know some people want to talk about how poor Jesus was, but that is the furthest thing from the truth.

When Jesus was born into the world, it didn't take long for Him to become very wealthy. When Jesus was around two years old, the wise men from the East came to His house with an abundance of treasures. The wise men were not just a couple of smart guys; according to history, these guys were king makers in the Middle East and extremely wealthy! They were responsible for putting kings on the thrones, and this is the reason that King Herod became very nervous when the wise men showed up.

The wise men didn't just show up with a little box of gold, frankincense, and myrrh. The wise men brought Jesus cargo loads full of treasures fit for a king. Based on the historical values of the items that were brought before the kings, a lower-level king would have received 110 kilos of gold (a monetary value today of $5 million dollars). But Jesus wasn't a lower-level king; Jesus was the King of kings, and what the wise men brought unto Jesus would have been a staggering amount.

This wealth not only sustained Mary and Joseph during their time in Egypt, but it also more than took care of them during Jesus' childhood, giving Jesus an abundance during His ministry. Jesus not only had a treasurer for His ministry, but He was also responsible for taking care of the twelve apostles and their families. You don't need a treasurer and twelve employees if you are broke! Even at Jesus' death, the soldiers were fighting over Jesus' clothes. Do you think the soldiers wanted some old beggar's clothes? No, Jesus' garments were that of a rich man, and the soldiers wanted them!

Jesus never begged for money and never went without. When Jesus was approached about His taxes, Jesus didn't have His treasurer with him; it was just Jesus and Peter. What did Jesus do? Did He take up an offering or have a telethon? No, He got a word from the Holy Spirit about where the needed money was and sent Peter to get it—out of a fish's mouth! Jesus paid for His taxes and Peter's taxes (see Matt. 17:24–27).

In the same way God sent Jesus into the world with abundance, Jesus sent you into the world with abundance. Jesus never meant for you to be in this world broke and barely getting by. It was never in Jesus' mind for His ministry representatives and His churches to be scraping by and barely surviving from one offering to another offering.

I've never understood preachers who preach God wants you humble and poor, and then they take up an offering. You can't give something you don't have!

Jesus needs you wealthy so you can be a blessing to the world and fulfill His call on your life.

It doesn't matter how anointed you are, without money, the anointing won't take you too far. When you buy real estate, food, clothes, vehicles, airtime, etc., those sellers expect payment in the form of money, not anointing. It takes spiritual equipment and physical equipment to get the job done. Thank God, you and I have everything, and I mean everything, that we need!

> *No one has risen into the heavenly realm except the Son of Man who also exists in heaven* (John 3:13 TPT).

> *Every spiritual blessing in the heavenly realm has already been lavished upon us as a love gift from our wonderful heavenly Father, the Father of our Lord Jesus—all because he sees us wrapped into Christ. This is why we celebrate him with all our hearts!* (Ephesians 1:3 TPT).

Just as Jesus was living out of Heaven while on the earth, you and I have that access and ability as well. Every resource Heaven has to offer is available to you through your union with Christ. It is time the Church starts viewing herself the way the Head of the Church viewed Himself while on the earth: fully supplied. God sent Jesus fully supplied, and in the very same way, Jesus sent us to manifest Heaven, and He equipped us with the spiritual and physical resources to fulfill the mission. Don't ever forget we have heaps upon heaps of grace to get the job done!

PRAYER

Jesus, thank You for trusting me enough to send me into this world to represent You. Holy Spirit, I ask You for greater clarity of my purpose on the earth. Give me a greater revelation of the authority and power that I have. I thank You for making all of Heaven's resources available for me. I will not lack for any good thing, and I will fulfill all You have called me to do!

Chapter 11

SET APART FOR OTHERS

*And for their sakes, I sanctify
Myself, that they also may be
sanctified by the truth* (John 17:19).

As Jesus continued praying in the upper room, He said, *"And for their sakes, I sanctify Myself."* Jesus had lived an extremely sanctified life. The word *sanctify* means "to set apart," and Jesus obviously lived a life that was very much set apart from the rest of the world. The life of Jesus was a life that was in the world, but not of the world—a life that produced supernatural results because of a continued renewal of the mind and intentional consciousness of God.

Jesus not only lived a sinless life, but He also lived a sanctified life. You may think it is the same, but it is not. You can live according to a list of rules and yet still have an unrenewed mind that sees impossibilities. Jesus was not just living right; He was thinking right. Jesus was continually sanctifying Himself by expanding His soul to what was possible with God. Jesus was continually stepping out and proving His dominion to Himself on the earth so He could show the disciples what was possible as a man filled with God. What led Jesus to live this way? Love.

Much can be said about His power, but love was the driving force of Jesus. His love for the Father drove Him not only to start the redemptive plan of God, but to finish it as well.

Jesus told the disciples, *My food is to do the will of Him who sent Me, and to finish His work* (John 4:34). We know how easy it is to start something and yet how difficult many times it is to see something through. Anyone can start a marathon, but not everyone finishes a marathon. There must be something inside you that pushes you to finish, and for Jesus, it was love. It was Jesus' love for the Father and love for humanity which fueled the fire within Him. Everything that Jesus did on the earth was initiated by love and sustained by love.

Love will make you do crazy things.

Love will cause you to set aside your plans.

Love will do what is best for the other person at a given time.

Love is self-sacrificing.

Love is giving your life so someone else can have a life.

Jesus said, *"For their sakes, I sanctify Myself, that they also may be sanctified by the truth."* Jesus had lived a sanctified life in order to be our sacrificial Lamb, but He also prepared to be the Altar and our High Priest. Jesus was willing to set aside His life so that we could live.

Too many times, we look at the sacrifice of Jesus as simply the forgiveness of sins and forget about the implications that come with the forgiveness of sins. To be forgiven is to be made the righteousness of God (see 2 Cor. 5:21). To be forgiven is to be healed (see 1 Pet. 2:24). To be forgiven is to be made a master over sin and sickness (see Romans 6:6). To be forgiven is to make satan your slave.

Jesus was willing to die so we could experience the life He was about to live!

> *Soon I will leave this world and they will see me no longer, but you will see me, because I will live again, and you will come alive too* (John 14:19 TPT).

Notice Jesus was talking to the disciples—these were human beings who were alive yet spiritual beings who were dead. Jesus' time of teaching in John 13–16 was all in the upper room as well. If you read through those chapters, you will find that in Jesus' last teaching moments with the disciples, He was talking to them about this supernatural life of union that would be available after salvation. Through salvation, they would become spiritually alive unto God!

And for their sakes, I sanctify Myself, that they also may be sanctified by the truth (John 17:19).

Notice the word *also*. In the same way Jesus was set apart, *we also* are to be set apart. Remember, this is all about union and sharing the same experience! To the very same degree that Jesus was in the world but not of the world, we are to be in the world but not of the world.

Jesus came so we could have life; but for us to have life, He had to give His life.

Jesus came so we could be in union with the Father; for us to have union with the Father, Jesus had to be separated from the Father. Jesus would not only die physically, but He would also die spiritually. I know some people get upset about this, but it is what it is. Jesus died spiritually on the cross because He had become sin.

For He made Him who knew no sin to be sin for us, so that we might become the righteousness of God in Him (2 Corinthians 5:21).

Jesus did not just take our sin; Jesus BECAME SIN. Jesus became the curse on the cross.

> *Yet, Christ paid the full price to set us free from the curse of the law. He absorbed the curse completely as He became a curse in our place. For it is written: "Everyone who is hung upon a tree is cursed"* (Galatians 3:13 TPT).

Through Jesus becoming sin and thus becoming the curse, He was dead spiritually. He was dead unto God and would have to pay the price for us in hell until the claims of justice were satisfied (see Rom. 4:25). At that moment, Jesus was born again!

> *For those whom He foreknew [and loved and chose beforehand], He also predestined to be conformed to the image of His Son [and ultimately share in His complete sanctification], so that He would be the firstborn [the most beloved and honored] among many believers* (Romans 8:29 AMP).

Jesus was not the first to be raised from the dead physically. Many people had been raised from the dead in the Old Testament, and we know for a fact that Jesus Himself raised at least three people from the dead! No, Jesus was the firstborn from among the spiritually dead. Glory! Jesus was the first. Jesus was the prototype of the new creation so that every single one who would come after would be absolutely perfect spirit beings!

> *And as members of the church of the Firstborn all our names have been legally registered as citizens of heaven! And we have come before God who judges all, and who lives among the spirits of the righteous who have been made perfect in his eyes!* (Hebrews 12:23 TPT).

Because of Jesus' sacrifice, we are in a position on the earth to be sanctified by the truth. Remember what the Greek word for *truth* means? Reality! Because of being perfect spirits made in His image and likeness, we can walk according to the realities of God. The will of God can now be made manifest perfectly through us on the earth. We can be like a superhero on this planet in which we walk unharmed through pandemics, live in continued prosperity despite famine, and live in absolute dominion over nature.

Jesus lived a sanctified life so that He was set apart as our sacrifice, and we can live according to the realities of God. Jesus showed us what was possible and then, through His sacrifice, removed the impossibilities that stood in our way so we could live according to the possibilities of God.

Not only does Jesus reveal His continued sanctification and the purpose of it, He also gives us the example of what we must do for others. Friend, we have all been called to the ministry of reconciliation (see 2 Cor. 5:18). For us to help bring people to God, we must know the way. We must continually and intentionally be renewing our minds according to the Kingdom of Heaven (see Rom. 12:2). We must continually and intentionally be setting our minds according to the realities of Heaven because we have died to this world (see Col. 3:1–3). In Christ, our spirits are perfect, but the process of sanctifying our souls is a continual one as Hebrews 10:14 tells us, *"For by one offering He has perfected forever those who are being sanctified."*

We must be separate enough for the world to see Jesus is the Way. We must be separate enough not only in our character but also in power. We must be walking according to this alternate reality in Him! We must be walking in the possibilities of God so the world can be sanctified according to His truth. Unfortunately, we must also do this for the modern Church, for there has never been a greater need for the Church to be sanctified unto the possibilities of God than in this day. The Church needs to be awakened—but it won't come through hype or entertainment. We can only awaken the spiritually alive in the Church and raise up the spiritually dead in the world by seeing ourselves in Christ and continually making the personal sacrifice of sanctifying ourselves unto His plan, His purpose, and His pursuits. Jesus made us perfect, but the sanctification process, the process of setting ourselves apart according to His reality, will continue through eternity.

Prayer

Father, I stand in awe of Your plan of redemption. Thank You for Your grace! Jesus, thank You for the sacrifices You made which allowed You to make the ultimate sacrifice for me. I ask for a greater revelation of redemption. Holy Spirit, open my eyes and help me to see with greater clarity all that Jesus provided for me. Help me to see who I truly am! I ask You to also help me to grow in my separateness from the world's systems so I can manifest Heaven. I ask for wisdom and revelation in this area so that I can also help bring others to this very same place of sanctification to God's realities.

Chapter 12

ONE WITH CHRIST

*I do not pray for these alone, but also for
those who will believe in Me through Your
word; that they all may be one, as You,
Father, are in Me, and I in You; that they
also may be one in Us, that the world may
believe that You sent Me* (John 17:20–21).

For the religious people who would listen to this
supernatural, prophetic prayer of Jesus and cast it off
as only for the apostles of His day, Jesus gets extremely
specific and lets us know He was praying these things
for every believer who would walk the earth. Jesus said
He was praying for *"those who will believe in Me."* If

we have accepted Jesus as our Lord and Savior, Jesus definitively lets us know He is praying these things for us.

In the entirety of the Gospels, if there is one statement Jesus made that stands out to me, it is John 17:21. The magnitude of what Jesus said here is mind-boggling to the carnal mind. After almost two decades of reading and studying it, it still gets to me every single time. For me, that verse is the weightiest scripture in the Bible and the most glorious statement to come out of Jesus' mouth. We see this truth relayed by the apostle Paul, but for me, I can almost see the glory of this flowing from Jesus' Spirit and out of His mouth, His heart full of joy knowing that what He had come to do was about to be fulfilled. The enormity of this marvelous miracle was simply days away, and its prophetic utterance had just been made.

Jesus said, *"Father, I pray that they would be one, just as You, Father, are in Me, and I in You; that they also may be one in Us."* Just looking at that right now—I still am amazed at the weight of that statement.

First, notice Jesus didn't initially pray that we would go to Heaven. Certainly, there is a Heaven to gain and a hell to shun. Heaven is a real place, and hell is a real place. I don't even want my enemies to go to hell, but the changing of our destination was not the primary focus of Jesus' mission. Jesus did not come to simply change our destination; Jesus came to change our position. Jesus did not simply come to take us somewhere; Jesus came to get God in us.

The crowning achievement of Jesus' life and ministry was the uniting of God and man. This union is not a prayer of individuals and groups living in unity. This was a declaration that not only would Jews and Gentiles become one new man, but that they would become one new man in union with the Father! Union was the plan of God from before the start of creation, and Jesus was the One bringing it to pass in the garden of Eden.

> *Then God said, "Let Us make man in Our image, according to Our likeness; let them have dominion over the fish of the sea, over the birds of the air, and over the cattle, over*

> *all the earth and over every creeping thing*
> *that creeps on the earth." So God created man*
> *in His own image; in the image of God He*
> *created him; male and female He created*
> *them. Then God blessed them, and God said*
> *to them, "Be fruitful and multiply; fill the*
> *earth and subdue it; have dominion over the*
> *fish of the sea, over the birds of the air, and*
> *over every living thing that moves on the*
> *earth"* (Genesis 1:26–27).

From the mind of God came the desire and plan to make man and woman in His image and likeness, and Jesus was right there hearing the command. Jesus received the word of God and brought it to pass; it was through Jesus that all things were made.

> *In the beginning the Living Expression was*
> *already there. And the Living Expression*
> *was with God, yet fully God. They were*
> *together—face-to-face, in the very begin-*
> *ning. And through his creative inspiration*
> *this Living Expression made all things,*

for nothing has existence apart from him!
(John 1:1–3 TPT).

The plan of God is fascinating, and the wisdom of God is astounding. In the garden, Jesus in His heavenly position and glory caused man to be like Them—the Godhead. Sadly, it didn't take long before Adam sinned and messed up God's perfect plan. Because of sin, Adam died spiritually, became separated from God, and thus sent the curse to run rampant through humanity. But thank God for Jesus! Jesus was there in the very beginning and saw everything unfold, but to fix Adam's mess, only a perfect, sinless One could be the substitute to redeem humanity. Jesus took on the mission Himself and came in human form. He started the job in the spirit as the Word four thousand years before in the garden of Eden; Jesus came in the flesh to finish the job as the Christ.

Do you see how powerful this is? He is the Author and the Finisher (see Heb. 12:2)! This is one reason it was so important for Jesus as His food was to finish the plan of God. Jesus' mission as the last Adam was to be the connector and bring God and man back together once again. However, this was going to be even better than before. Not only would we be made in the image and likeness of God—we would be united with Him! This would be a covenant that was foolproof. This would not be a covenant made with God and man; this was a covenant made between God and God! Because of Jesus being the Great Substitute, He took on the price of our redemption. In the eyes of justice, when Jesus died, we died, and when Jesus was raised up, we were raised up. As a result, the union Jesus had automatically become ours when we received Him as our Savior and were born again. Never again could man be the cause of undoing the union of God and man again. God is brilliant!

Jesus knew that union with God would make us spiritually alive again. Notice what Jesus told the disciples before He began to pray this supernatural prayer in the upper room.

> *A little while longer and the world will see Me no more, but you will see Me. Because I live, you will live also. At that day you will*

*know that I am in My Father, and you in
Me, and I in you* (John 14:19–20).

Jesus and the disciples were in the upper room in
their physical bodies, very much alive—and yet Jesus
basically said, "On the day I live, you will live also."
Jesus was prophesying about the day He would rise up
as the Firstborn from the spiritually dead; as a result
of Him becoming alive after becoming the curse, the
disciples would come alive as well. Again, this wasn't
referring to physically becoming alive; this was referring to spiritually becoming alive. The disciples were
alive in the flesh but dead in the spirit; however, in
a few short days, the life that flowed in Jesus would
flow in them, and they would share in the very same
connection with God that Jesus had.

In the very way Jesus was alive unto God, we were
to be alive unto God. The fellowship Adam had with
God in the garden and Jesus had on the earth is available to us as well. All that flowed in God could now
flow through us. The life Jesus lived on the earth was
the very same life we can live on the earth.

For he knew all about us before we were born and he destined us from the beginning to share the likeness of his Son. This means the Son is the oldest among a vast family of brothers and sisters who will become just like him (Romans 8:29 TPT).

God's plan of making man in His image and likeness was once again back in play! Jesus was the firstborn among many brothers and sisters. Essentially, what happened on the day of salvation was what happened in the garden of Eden; however, instead of making Adam, God made a new creation in Christ so that through Christ all that would come would be absolutely perfect.

You could say that Jesus was the prototype! In manufacturing, before any product can be mass produced, there must be a prototype. When God decided what He wanted this new creation to look like, He fashioned Jesus according to that manner so that everyone who came after Jesus would be exactly like Him (see 2 Cor. 5:17). Everything that God wanted man to be,

He made Jesus to be. Everything God wanted in man, He put into Jesus. Everything God wanted man to be able to do on the earth, God enabled Jesus to do. Certainly, we would still have our own personalities, but we would share in His righteousness, glory, healing, and dominion.

I know this is a hard truth for our little brains, but we must renew our minds to the reality of redemption. The reason we have a hard time seeing ourselves in union with Him is because we are very flesh conscious. We have not renewed our minds to the things of Heaven; instead, too many of us are ruled by our bodies. Most Christians still see themselves as sinners saved by grace. Friend, you can't be a sinner and be saved by grace. You can't have two identities; you are either saved by grace, or you are a sinner—even the world understands you can't have two identities! The world calls it a dissociative identity disorder, but the Church sees it as normal! The more you understand that you are a spirit being, the easier it will make things for you. When you understand you are a spirit with a soul that is living in a body, you'll stop identifying with the body. You'll stop allowing the body to tell you who you are in Christ and what you can do for Christ. You'll stop living in condemnation and stop living in self-righteousness.

The powerful reality of our union with Christ is the thread that runs through all the apostle Paul's letters to the churches. It is the theme of the new covenant and the foundation from which every blessing of God flows. You will never truly walk in all God has for you until you know this magnificent truth.

If you want to know what you are like, simply look at Jesus. As Jesus is, so are we in this world (see 1 John 4:17). It is in Him that we live and move and have our being (see Acts 17:28). It is in Christ that we are complete (see Col. 2:10). It is in Christ that we can do all things (see Phil. 4:13). It is in Christ we always triumph (see 2 Cor. 2:14). It is in Christ that we have been brought near unto God (see Eph. 2:13). It is in Christ we have all the blessings of Heaven (see Eph. 1:3).

If there ever was one truth a new believer should understand, it is the reality of union. For me, it is the first thing I begin teaching a new Christian, and even after being saved for forty years, it is still the subject I major on. Many know me for the ministry of healing, but hang around me for a short time, and you will find out quickly that union is what I focus on and even what I preach in our healing conferences and crusades. It is the message I have been called to preach and help restore to the Church in these last days. Jesus lived for, prayed for, died for, and was raised up for this reality; therefore, it should be our focus. If you want miracles, if you want churches in constant revival, and if you want Christians with high morals and upstanding character, teach them about their union with Christ.

For centuries, preachers focused on beating the hell out of Christians. Even in churches today, the focus is on sin—but do you know what happens when you constantly preach on sin? You produce Christians who are good at sinning! Instead of telling them what not to do, tell them WHO THEY ARE! When the Christian understands who they are in Christ, the sinful life will melt away because they will begin to operate according to grace and die to the life of works.

PRAYER

God, thank You for Your infinite wisdom and for not giving up on Your plan. Jesus, thank You for the sacrifice You made so I could be in union with You, the Father, and the Holy Spirit. I humbly accept who You made me to be. I ask You as the Head of the Church to help me to see all that I am in You. Holy Spirit, open my eyes and reveal to me the wonder of my union with the Godhead and all that was made available to me through this precious reality of union that was sealed by the blood of Jesus Christ.

Chapter 13

THE SAME GLORY

*And the glory which You gave Me I
have given them, that they may be
one just as We are one* (John 17:22).

Throughout Jesus' prayer, we see the uniting of God
and man as the cry of the Godhead. It was the plan
of God before the foundation of the world, and Jesus
fulfilled that plan and sealed it forever with His blood.
As Jesus continued to pray, He declared another radical truth that elevates even more the Christian position and experience. Jesus said, *"The glory which You
gave Me I have given them."*

Just that statement makes the religious people shake in their shoes! Imagine standing in a church and declaring, "The same glory that Jesus has, I have!"—do you realize most Christians would call you a heretic? But these were not the words of some famous television preacher or a particular denomination; these are the words of Jesus Himself! Either we choose to believe them, or we choose to throw them out. Religion will find some way to water down this message or eliminate it completely because religious folk question the audacity of someone seeing himself in the same way as Jesus! Friend, stinking, rotten, demonic pride will have you see yourself through a lens of unrighteousness! You must remember that it was God's idea to make you righteous and one with Him.

So, it is obvious from the mouth of Jesus that Jesus gave us the glory the Father gave Him, but what is this glory?

The glory of God carries a tremendous amount of weight throughout the Bible. This word *glory* is used a total of 340 times in the Bible. In Hebrew, it is the word *kavod*, and it means "glory, honor, abundance, riches, and splendor" and yet can be translated as "the heavyweight of God's presence that is filled with everything that is good."[8]

The first mentions of "the glory of God" are in Exodus 16, which says,

> *And in the morning you shall see the glory of the Lord. . . . Now it came to pass, as Aaron spoke to the whole congregation of the children of Israel, that they looked toward the wilderness, and behold, the glory of the Lord appeared in the cloud* (vv. 7, 10).

One of the more well-known passages is Exodus 33, in which Moses cried out, *"God, show me Your glory!"*

> *And he said, "Please, show me Your glory." Then He said, "I will make all My goodness pass before you, and I will proclaim the name of the Lord before you. I will be gracious to whom I will be gracious, and I will have compassion on whom I will have compassion"* (Exodus 33:18–19).

Notice that God equates His glory with His goodness; however, God didn't just tell Moses about His goodness—God showed Moses His goodness! The glory of God brought the goodness of God, and it was to be experienced!

We also find out that when Solomon dedicated the temple, the Presence of God filled the temple to such a degree that the priests could not even stand up!

> *So that the priests could not stand to minister because of the cloud: for the glory of the Lord had filled the house of the Lord* (1 Kings 8:11).

You may have experienced something similar yourself. You may have been in church services when the Presence of God was manifest to such a degree that it was hard to stand up. There have been many times I have been ministering when the Presence of God became so strong that I had to grab hold of something to keep myself steady. This same glory of the Presence of God has caused people to fall down when someone has ministered to them by the laying on of hands. Why? Because the goodness of God is just that magnificent!

Notice every time the glory of God shows up, encounters with God take place—and it is always good! Isaiah prophesied,

> *Arise, shine; for your light has come, and the glory of the Lord is risen upon you. For behold, the darkness shall cover the earth, and deep darkness the people; but the Lord shall arise over you, and His glory will be seen upon you* (Isaiah 60:1–2).

This is what happened when Moses got into the Presence of God on the mountain. The Presence of God got into his skin, and Moses began to shine with light! Another aspect of the glory of God is light! Light will not only illuminate, but it will also purify, heal, cleanse, and instantly drive out darkness.

We find over and over again the glory of God, or you could say the Presence of God was always meant to be experienced whether it be seen or felt.

When we get over into the New Testament, we find the word *glory* used in the very same way. The Greek word for *glory* is *doxa* and means "glory, brightness, honorable, and magnificent."[9]

When we look at the life of Jesus, it is interesting that the glory is never mentioned until after Jesus was anointed by the Holy Spirit in the Jordan River. When the Holy Spirit came upon Jesus, miracles began to happen in Jesus' life and ministry. The glory of God had been within Jesus, and then the glory was upon Jesus, equipping Him for ministry.

> *This miracle in Cana was the first of the many extraordinary miracles Jesus performed in Galilee that revealed his glory, and his disciples believed in him* (John 2:11 TPT).

Where you find the glory, you find miracles because the life of God and the light of God are there! Mankind was made to experience God's glory. More specifically, the glory of God was the clothing of Adam and Eve before they sinned; they were clothed in the magnificence and goodness of God! We were originally made for God's Presence.

> *For all have sinned and fall short of the glory of God, being justified freely by His grace through the redemption that is in Christ Jesus, whom God set forth as a propitiation by His blood, through faith, to demonstrate His righteousness, because in His forbearance God had passed over the sins that were previously committed, to demonstrate at the present time His righteousness, that He might be just and the justifier of the one who has faith in Jesus* (Romans 3:23–26).

Because of Adam's sin, Adam went from living in the glory of God to living outside it; every man born after Adam was in need of the glory of God but couldn't access it.

Many Christians know Romans 3:23 but take it out of context because the apostle Paul wasn't focusing on sin; if you read the rest of his statements, the apostle Paul was focusing on righteousness. He was letting us know the good news that even though we were born into sin and lacking the glory of God, because of salvation, we become the righteousness of God and have full access to the glory! Jesus essentially said, "Father, the glory You gave Me, I have given them!" This was the mystery of the gospel! Through salvation, our old sinful self died, and we were made righteous and given back the glory of God because of Christ in us!

> For God wanted them to know that the riches and glory of Christ are for you Gentiles, too. And this is the secret: Christ lives in you. This gives you assurance of sharing His glory (Colossians 1:27 NLT).

Why can we expect to experience the glory of God? Because of our union with Christ! Do you see why union is so important? What was the secret that was hidden for generations and generations? CHRIST IN YOU. And what would be the result? THE GLORY OF GOD IN YOU! It is impossible for us to be one with Him and not share in what He has.

And the Word became flesh and dwelt among us, and we beheld His glory, the glory as of the only begotten of the Father, full of grace and truth. . . . And of His fullness we have all received, and grace for grace (John 1:14, 16).

I want you to get this. Jesus did not give you just a little bit of glory. Jesus didn't give you just a little bit of the Presence of God! Of His fullness we have all received! You can't be in union with something and not share the same stuff.

If you were to take the cord of a lamp and plug it into an electrical socket, not only would they become one, but the power flowing in the socket would then be the same power flowing in the cord. It is impossible for them to become connected and yet not share in the same power. This was another reason Jesus needed us to become righteous! Jesus needed us to be perfect in spirit so we could be united with Him and thus share in the same glory! Jesus needed us to have the same degree of the light of God, the life of God, the goodness of God, and the power of God to continue destroying the works of darkness on the earth and manifesting Heaven. How would that happen? By us having the glory of God!

> *For now he towers above all creation, for all things exist through him and for him. And that God made him, pioneer of our salvation, perfect through his sufferings, for this is how he brings many sons and daughters to share in his glory* (Hebrews 2:10 TPT).

Now, understandably, some people would say, "So, if we have the same glory Jesus had, why aren't we experiencing it the same way?" Well, first of all, you can't experience what you don't know that you have. Most Christians will see in Scripture that they may have some of what Jesus has, but because of religious pride, they would never see themselves fully having what Jesus has.

Satan has used religion as a way to trick and deceive Christians to think they don't have enough. However, IT IS IMPOSSIBLE for you to be one with Christ and not share in what He has. Not only that IT IS IMPOSSIBLE for you to do the same works as Jesus and even greater works and yet have less equipment! It amazes me that Christians will talk about doing the same works as Jesus but think they have less authority, power, and anointing—but that makes no sense! Are you telling me I am supposed to do what Jesus did and somehow pull that off with less anointing and power?

We do not have an equipment problem; we have an awareness problem. The more aware of who we are in Jesus and what we have, the more we will find ourselves walking in greater glory.

> *But we all, with unveiled face, beholding as in a mirror the glory of the Lord, are being transformed into the same image from glory to glory, just as by the Spirit of the Lord* (2 Corinthians 3:18).

The phrase *"from glory to glory"* is talking about greater dimensions. All of it has been made available, but all of it cannot be accessed until we begin to expand our souls. The more we begin to see ourselves according to His image and His glory, the more we will be changed and step into another dimension of glory.

This is to be a continuous process of walking into greater dimensions while we are on the earth! How does this happen? By continually looking at Jesus!

You'll never walk in greater dimensions of glory while you are looking in your natural mirror. Day and night, you must meditate on who you are in Christ so that all of Christ can live through you.

Prayer

Father, I want to walk in greater glory! I see that the glory You gave Jesus has been given to me. I realize I am walking so far short of what has been made available, and I do not want to take the sacrifice of Jesus in vain. I desire to walk in the fullness of Your grace! Holy Spirit, open my eyes and help me to see who I am. Whatever things in my life that are holding me down and holding me back, I ask You to reveal them to me. Help me to continually be transformed and go into higher dimensions of Your glory so I can bring You greater glory by manifesting a higher glory on the earth.

Chapter 14

"THAT THE WORLD MAY KNOW"

I in them, and You in Me; that they
may be made perfect in one, and that
the world may know that You have
sent Me, and have loved them as
You have loved Me (John 17:23).

T he crowning achievement of Jesus' life and ministry was the unifying of God and man. This was the joy set before Jesus that enabled Him to endure the cross and the shame. We see this as He prayed unto God, *"I in them, and You in Me."* As Jesus was praying,

He made two statements that would basically get you kicked out of most churches if you got up and preached them.

First, Jesus said, *"I in them, and You in me; that they would be perfect in one."* Through salvation, Jesus made you the righteousness of God. Jesus made you just as right as God. Jesus made you perfect. I have literally had people say, "Chad, who do you think you are? Only Jesus alone was perfect." Well, I must agree that Jesus alone is perfect; however, I know who I am—I am a man in Christ, and that makes me perfect!

I know that it is a radical statement. Most of the Church would have a major problem with you calling yourself perfect; most Christians would call it pride, but God would call it humble! Do you know why? Because it takes humility to believe what God has called you and made you! When you begin to see yourself as a spirit united with the Father of spirits, it makes it easier to see yourself as perfect.

I love Hebrews 10:14 because it reveals that even in our mess: *"For by one offering He has perfected for-ever those who are being sanctified."* We have been made like our Messiah. Certainly, we are not perfect in our minds and emotions and flesh, but our souls and flesh are not us—we are spirits. Our spirits are the real us that are made in the likeness and image of God. Our spirits have been made perfect. Remember, when you are born again, you are made in His image and likeness—you are made the righteousness of God! God is perfect; therefore, how could He unite Himself with someone who is imperfect with even the tiniest imperfection? He can't! You must be absolutely perfect in even the minutest way to be united to God. Friend, that is what righteousness is all about!

Notice also that Jesus perfected *forever* those who are being sanctified. This is a radical truth that we must grasp as it will keep us out of condemnation and keep us manifesting Heaven. Even while we are working out our salvation, we are perfect in Christ. Even while we are continually renewing our minds and expanding our souls, we are perfect in Christ. Forever you are perfect in Him! How is that possible? Because you were made righteous!

For God made the only one who did not know sin to become sin for us, so that we might become the righteousness of God through our union with him (2 Corinthians 5:21 TPT).

You were not just given righteousness like a package put in your hand. Certainly, righteousness is a gift, but righteousness is not an item; it is something you become. Righteousness becomes part of your identity! He made you perfect. This means your actions have nothing to do with who you are. Now, I know some people would get upset and look at that statement as a license to sin—but it is not. When you truly understand what God has made you to be, you don't want to sin; in reality, it empowers you to dominate sin!

And as members of the church of the Firstborn all our names have been legally registered as citizens of heaven! And we have come before God who judges all, and who lives among the spirits of the righteous who have been made perfect in his eyes! (Hebrews 12:23 TPT).

This is a reality that the Church is still struggling to grasp—but we must! Stop looking at yourself through your eyes; look at yourself through His eyes because He sees you, the spirit being, as perfect.

This leads me to the second part of Jesus' statement in John 17:23—*"That the world may know that You have sent Me."* Jesus actually prayed this same declaration in verse 21:

> *That they all may be one, as You, Father, are in Me, and I in You; that they also may be one in Us, that the world may believe that You sent Me.*

Here we go with more truth bombs! As if Jesus' first statement about you being made perfect weren't profound, Jesus went ahead and took it to another level of extreme! Jesus more or less said, "I pray they would be perfect in one so that the world would know You sent Me." Now friend, how would the world know that God sent Jesus simply by seeing you? Take a moment and think about that question. Is your brain spinning right now? Get ready for a revolutionary statement: because when they see you, they are supposed to see Him.

I know that religion starts to creep up and yell, "Who do you think you are?" Well, that's what I am trying to help us understand by looking at what Jesus prayed. Now don't get mad at me; Jesus made the statement! Jesus is the One who prayed, "Father, let them be perfect so the world would know you sent Me!"

God made you to be so perfect, so perfect in your union with Christ, that you should be an exact reflection of Him. There should be such a radical difference in your life compared to the world, that the sinner could see what grace had done. In reality, we should be able to tell people, "If you have seen me, you have seen the Christ!" I get eye rolls from people when I talk about it, but I don't care anymore. Jesus is the One who prayed it and made it happen—not me!

It is funny, though, because I grew up going to youth conferences in a certain mainline denomination, and all I heard was, "You may be the only Jesus people ever see." There was a truth they were telling us, but they didn't realize the extent of that truth. They were only looking at it from the perspective of our character and love walk. Certainly, we should have the highest character in the world. We should walk in honor toward our teachers, employers, political leaders, and all those who are in authority over us. We should walk in love toward all of those around us. We should do good to those who are less fortunate and be a blessing whenever we have the opportunity—but sinners can do that.

You don't need to be born again to give a handout; evil people do that all the time simply for a tax write-off! There is more to walking in love than doing good things; the world needs a Church that manifests the love of God in power! The love of God will compel you and empower you to heal the sick, raise the dead, cleanse the leper, and cast out the devil! The world needs the glory and the anointing of the Christ in action, and yet they will only experience it when you allow Jesus to manifest through your union with Him.

In Genesis 2:7, God formed the body of Adam and then put Adam into the body. Many rabbis teach that when God created Adam, all of the angels watching initially could not tell which one was God and which one was Adam? Why? Because Adam was made like God and clothed in His glory! Honestly, I don't have a problem with that teaching because it lines up with Genesis 1:26 where God said, *"Let us make man in Our image and likeness!"* Even when Jesus walked on the earth, Jesus was bold enough to say, *"If you have seen Me, you have seen the Father!"*

> *Jesus replied, "Philip, I've been with you all this time and you still don't know who I am? How could you ask me to show you the Father, for anyone who has looked at me has seen the Father. Don't you believe that the Father is living in me and that I am living in the Father? Even my words are not my own but come from my Father, for he lives in me and performs his miracles of power through me. Believe that I live as one with my Father and that my Father lives as one with me—or at least, believe because of the mighty miracles I have done* (John 14:9–11 TPT).

Do you see this? While Jesus was in the upper room with the disciples, He said, "If you have seen Me, you have seen the Father; He lives in Me and I live in Him." Union with Christ is a reflection of Christ; not only that to be one with Him produces the miracles of Him!

Jesus equated being one with the Father to the miracles people were seeing. Jesus didn't say that giving money to the poor proved His union with the Father. Jesus didn't say that clothing the naked proved His union with the Father. Jesus didn't say that all of His social services proved His union with the Father. Jesus said the miracles proved His union with the Father!

The world is groaning and waiting for the revealing of the true sons and daughters of God. Listen to me very clearly: There will be no last-day awakening without the Church knowing this vital truth. When you see your perfection in Him, it will give you great confidence to stand against the curse of the world and set the captive free. Not only will captives experience Jesus, but they will experience the love God has for them. Without knowing this, the Church will not be able to operate in the power to the degree God intended. You cannot walk in the glory of Christ if you don't know you have it. Yes, we have seen smatterings of power here and there over the years, but nothing like Jesus had planned.

We are not waiting on God to give us something extra; you will not find that type of prayer in the Bible. You would not find Jesus praying the same prayers that much of the modern Church prays. Much of the modern Church is praying for more, but when you look at what Jesus prayed and then accomplished through His death, burial, and resurrection—what is left for God to give?

Yes, there is much more to walk in, but Jesus tore the door off the hinges to the warehouse of Heaven and made it all available to you through your union in Him (see Eph. 1:3). Jesus is the Way! What we walk in is according to what we access. The degree of power and anointing we walk in and demonstrate will be directly tied to our experiential understanding of our union with Christ—for it is the foundation of which the fruit of Heaven is dispensed.

Prayer

Father, thank You for making me righteous. Help me to see myself the way You see me. May the miracle-working power of Jesus be experienced in its fullness through my life— not for my glory but for Your glory. I vow this day to walk according to Your image and Your likeness and to see myself through Your eyes so the world will see You. I pray for wisdom and revelation as to who I am in You so the world will know that You sent Jesus. Holy Spirit, I yield myself to You, as the perfect vessel that I am, to be a conduit of Your power like my generation has never seen before. Let the lightnings of God flash through my soul, and Your exceedingly great glory push back the darkness with every step that I take. May the world encounter the fullness of You through me.

Chapter 15

TO BE WITH JESUS

*Father, I desire that they also whom You
gave Me may be with Me where I am,
that they may behold My glory which You
have given Me; for You loved Me before
the foundation of the world* (John 17:24).

As we have seen before, Jesus' ultimate desire was the union of God and man. Jesus' primary focus was not to change our destination but to change our position; however, by changing our position, our destination was changed as well. When you look at how dominant we have made Heaven the focus of the Christian experience, it is quite amazing in comparison to where

Jesus places it. During this entire time of prayer and prophecy, Jesus never mentioned a change in destination until verse 24 when He essentially said, "Father, I desire that those You gave Me would be with Me where I am."

Thank God for Heaven. I have seen a small portion of it, and I won't lie, but I didn't want to come back; earth, my family and my friends weren't even on my mind. In October of 2005, I had been spending some extra time in prayer for a few weeks and started having some incredible supernatural experiences. One night, I laid down to go to sleep, and the next thing I knew, I was in Heaven. The first thing that stood out to me was not my surroundings, but what I felt in my body. There was a peace I had never experienced before, but also a continuous surge of electricity pulsated through my body. It didn't hurt, but I could feel it. The only way I know how to explain it would be like putting a TENS unit on your body and feeling the light but very tangible electric current flowing in your muscles. I was very, very aware of the life of God that was flowing in me. I then looked around and saw people walking and children playing. To my left, I saw a building just a few feet from me; I walked in the door, and there stood Jesus.

We talked for a while, and then we walked outside. As we walked out the door, a massive crowd of people walked down the road and exclaimed, "It's time to go to the throne room! It's time to go to the throne room!" There was much excitement in the multitude of people. I got so excited about it that I took off running, trying to get ahead of the crowd. We then approached a staircase, and I began running up the staircase to be the first in line. When I reached the top of the staircase, I came to a door. When I went through the door, to my amazement, there was God on His throne. I could see everything about Him except for His face; I could see His smile, but a haze covered the upper portion of His face. I won't go into detail about the entire experience, but let me tell you that Heaven is real!

I am thankful that when I fulfill the plan of God for my life and am satisfied with the years I have lived, I can take my last breath on the earth and go to Heaven. That experience and other experiences have made me look very lightly on the things of the earth. It also changed my perspective on death; I began to see where we had made death a big deal when, in reality, it is not a big deal at all. Death is simply our letting go of the body so we can get a massive upgrade!

However, let us put things in the proper perspective. If Jesus were to come today, we would be in Heaven for seven years during the tribulation. After the tribulation, all of us would return to the earth for the 1,000-year reign of Christ. After the thousand years, satan would finally be cast into the lake of fire, the earth that we know would be burned up and remade, and then Heaven would come down and become part of the new earth. So, this is less about going to Heaven and more about being with Jesus. Remember, all of this is about relationship and fellowship with Him!

I want to bring your attention to some other statements Jesus made in the upper room before He began to pray.

"Let not your heart be troubled; you believe in God, believe also in Me. In My Father's house there are many mansions; if it were not so, I would have told you. I go to prepare a place for you. And if I go and prepare a place for you, I will come again and receive you to Myself; that where I am, there you may be also. And where I go you know, and the way you know." Thomas said to Him, "Lord, we do not know where You are going, and how can we know the way?" Jesus said to him, "I am the way, the truth, and the life. No one comes to the Father except through Me" (John 14:1–6).

Jesus was obviously talking about going somewhere. It was a change in destination. Jesus was talking about when we shed our earthly bodies, take on our spiritual bodies, and are physically with Him.

Although I look forward to that time in the future, let us not forget about the present; there is more to this than what we realize.

Although Jesus said, "I'm going and coming again," Jesus also said, "Where I go you know and the way you know." Look at something else Jesus said in this same time of teaching.

> Soon I will leave this world and they will see me no longer, but you will see me, because I will live again, and you will come alive too. So when that day comes, you will know that I am living in the Father and that you are one with me, for I will be living in you. Those who truly love me are those who obey my commands. Whoever passionately loves me will be passionately loved by my Father. And I will passionately love him in return and will reveal myself to him (John 14:19–21 TPT).

The word *reveal* is the Greek word *emphanizo* which means "to manifest, exhibit to view, to show one's self, come to view, appear, be manifest."[10] This Greek word is used ten times in the New Testament; four times it refers to someone disclosing information, and six times it refers to a showing, display, or appearance of something or someone. In the Septuagint, Moses declared, "*If then I have found favour in thy sight, reveal thyself to me, that I may evidently see thee; that I may find favour in thy sight, and that I may know that this great nation thy people*" (Exodus 33:13). What was the result of Moses' request? God put Moses in the cleft of the rock and allowed Moses to see His glory.

With all that background information, clearly, Jesus was not simply talking about the sharing of information; this is about divine manifestations. I like Dr. Brian Simmons' note on this verse from the Passion Translation: "I . . . will reveal myself to him" is more than merely "showing him who I am." It means "I will personally come to him."

Jesus was letting the disciples know that even though He would physically be leaving and preparing a place for them, this would not be the end of their encounters with Him.

> *Soon I will leave this world and they will see me no longer, but you will see Me, because*

> *I will live again, and you will come alive*
> *too. So when that day comes, you will know*
> *that I am living in the Father and that you*
> *are one with me, for I will be living in you*
> (John 14:19–20 TPT).

Jesus told them that on the day of salvation, they will come alive. Jesus wasn't talking to people who were physically dead; He was talking to people who were spiritually dead! Jesus was letting them know that when they became spiritually alive, they would come alive unto God. Because they would be alive unto God, they would *know* of their union with God and His indwelling Presence. This word *know* is not simply referring to intellectual knowledge; this is about experiential knowledge. Again, we are seeing a truth here that just because Jesus would be gone physically, there would still be the promise of encounters with Him. How? Because we would be spiritually alive and in union with Him.

We are told in Acts 2 that because of the Holy Spirit being poured out, we would experience dreams and visions. I do not believe this was just for information. Thank God for such experiences, but I also firmly believe these were for supernatural encounters with the glorified Christ as well. In His last teaching session with the disciples, Jesus very plainly lets them know, "I am going to be leaving the earth and going to Heaven, but even though I may not be here physically, I will still manifest Myself to you." One day, we will physically be with Jesus, but while we are waiting, we can still "be with Him" spiritually. We can know the glorified Christ here on the earth because Jesus made the way.

I know this may sound a little farfetched, but these are the words of Jesus Himself. Maybe you are one of many who would say, "I see what Jesus said. But if it is true, how come I haven't had any real spiritual encounters and experiences?" Well, it is a legitimate question, and my response would simply be this: "Maybe it's because church folk told us it wasn't possible."

Instead of listening to what small-minded Christians are saying, maybe we should start listening to what Jesus was saying. Jesus is the One who said, "The world will see Me no longer but you will see Me." Jesus is the One who said, "I will reveal Myself to You." Jesus is the One who said, "You know the way." Jesus is the One who said, "On that day, you will know by experience that I am in the Father, the Father is in Me and I am in You." Instead of taking the words of Jesus and endeavoring to squeeze them into our religious boxes, let us take the words of Jesus for face value, expand our souls, and find out what is possible. Why? Because Jesus wants you to know Him.

PRAYER

Jesus, You are the Way. Thank You for making the way for me to be with You in Heaven. Let the reality of Heaven and eternity with You become greater in Me. Holy Spirit, I ask You for a more heavenly perspective of life and death. Help me to renew my mind, develop my soul, and expand my faith for encounters with You. Jesus, I take off the limits today, and I declare that visions, dreams, and supernatural encounters with You will be my normal.

Chapter 16

"I Have Known You"

O righteous Father! The world
has not known You, but I have
known You; and these have known
that You sent Me (John 17:25).

As if Jesus had not already made some eye-open-
ing statements, what Jesus said while He was praying
verse 25 is probably one of the biggest shock statements of all. Jesus said, "*The world has not known You,*
but I have known You." Now, if you read that from the
perspective of Jesus saying this as God on the earth,

then it isn't that big of a deal; however, if you read this statement as Jesus saying this as a Man on the earth—this is a massive deal!

Remember, this word *know* is the Greek word *ginosko*, which is talking about experiential knowledge; Jesus wasn't saying that He knew facts about the Father. Jesus was saying that as a Man on the earth, He knew the Father. If the magnitude of this statement isn't hitting you yet, look at what else Jesus said regarding this reality:

> *As the Father knows Me, even so I know the Father; and I lay down My life for the sheep* (John 10:15).

Do you see it? *"As the Father knows Me, even so I know the Father."* Jesus said that as a Man with a brain like you and a body like you. Jesus was saying this as a human being. It doesn't get any bigger than this!

Jesus was letting the Jews know that He knew God the Father in the same way you would know your spouse, children, or very best friend. Jesus didn't just know about God; Jesus knew God—as a Man!

Did Jesus know God simply by knowing Scriptures? Not necessarily. The Scribes and Pharisees knew the Law and the Prophets factually just as much as Jesus did. Jesus actually told the Pharisees, *"You search the Scriptures for in them you think there is eternal life and these are they which testify of Me"* (John 5:39). Jesus wasn't discounting the Scriptures; Jesus was letting them know they did not have revelation of the Scriptures.

It wasn't simply having revelation of Scripture, however, that helped Jesus know the Father. Revelation of the Scripture actually led Jesus into a fellowship with the Father. Remember, Jesus was doing life as a Man; Jesus was doing life just like you and me. There is a reason Jesus had to be anointed by the Holy Spirit. Why? Because Jesus was doing life as a Man; God doesn't need to be anointed! The apostle Paul told the Philippian church that Jesus set aside His glory and all that gave Him an advantage, and He humbled Himself and came to the earth as a Man (see Phil. 2:5–6). Luke tells us that Jesus grew not only in stature, but also in wisdom (see Luke 2:52).

God doesn't grow in wisdom, but men do! Jesus also told us in John 5:20 that God was going to show Him even greater things than He had seen before. This also reveals that Jesus did not know everything but was learning and growing in revelation just as we do.

Why is this important? Because if I see Jesus do life as God, His statements cause me to only praise Him, but if I see Jesus do life as a Man anointed by God, it inspires and compels me to do what He did. When Jesus says, *"O righteous Father, I know You,"* it reveals that I can know the Father in the very same way.

Remember, Jesus didn't just know Scriptures; Jesus knew God. Jesus knew God like you know your very best friend. How do you get to know your friend? Through fellowship.

Look at some of the things Jesus said about His fellowship with the Father, and read this from the perspective of Jesus saying these things as a Man.

> *I speak to you eternal truth. The Son is unable*
> *to do anything from himself or through his*
> *own initiative. I only do the works that I see*

the Father doing, for the Son does the same works as his Father. Because the Father loves his Son so much, he always reveals to him everything that he is about to do. And you will all be amazed when he shows him even greater works than what you've seen so far! (John 5:19–20 TPT).

Nothing I do is from my own initiative. As I hear the judgment passed by my Father, I execute those judgments. And my judgments will be perfect, because I seek only to fulfill the desires of my Father who sent me (John 5:30 TPT).

For I am the only One who has come from the Father's side, and I have seen the Father! (John 6:46 TPT).

The Father has sent me here, and I know all about him, for I have come from his presence (John 7:29 TPT).

And I still have many more things to pronounce in judgment about you. For I will

> *testify to the world of the truths that I have heard from my Father, and the Father who sent me is trustworthy* (John 8:26 TPT).
>
> *I've only told you the truth that I've heard in my Father's presence, but now you are wanting me dead—is that how Abraham acted?* (John 8:40 TPT).

When you read these statements from Jesus, it is wildly apparent Jesus' fellowship with God went way beyond reading Scripture. Jesus was seeing and hearing from the Father and spending time with Him in His Presence. When you read these scriptures (and there are many more), you begin to see that Jesus' relationship with the Father was just as real as His relationship with Peter, James, John, or anyone else. I don't know about you, but when I read these things, it not only makes me jealous of what Jesus had, but also inspires me to have it as well.

The last few years of my life, I have become completely unsatisfied with my Christian experience in a good way. I am so thankful for all that I have experienced and the miracles I have seen firsthand. I have literally watched tumors dissolve under my hand, short legs and arms grow out, blind and deaf healed, skin diseases just fade away, people get out of wheelchairs, broken bones mend, and it all has been awesome! As fun as that has been, it hasn't been enough. It started out that I just wanted to see miracles. Over time, it developed into wanting to help people, and while that is still the case, now I ultimately just want to know Him.

The more I see Jesus' relationship with the Father and then see that it's available to me, it is all that I want now. I am like the apostle Paul in that I want to not just know the power—I want to know Him (see Phil. 3:10). The entire Christian experience is all about relationship and fellowship. It was the entire reason Jesus came to unite us with Him—so that we would be spiritually alive again and could have unhindered fellowship. Fellowship with man was God's plan from the very beginning! God made Adam in His image and likeness and clothed him in His glory so they could walk and talk together. Our fellowship with

God wasn't to simply be limited to knowing Scripture; the purpose of the Scripture was to lead us into a fellowship of knowing Him!

And so, Jesus told the disciples in the upper room, "The world will see Me no more, but you will see Me. On that day, you will know that I am in the Father, the Father is in Me and I am in you. I will love you and I will reveal Myself to you." Do you see it? This should cause your heart to begin to pound and excitement to be stirred up within you.

Because of our union with Christ, the very same fellowship Jesus had with the Father, we can have with the Father. He can be just as real to you as your very best friend! The things of Heaven should be even more real to us! Just as we have five physical senses, we have five spiritual senses. We are spirit beings united to the Father of our spirits.

Jesus opened the door. Jesus wants you to know Him just as He knows you!

PRAYER

O righteous Father, I thank You that I know You, but I want to know You even more! I refuse to settle with simply knowing facts about You; I desire to know You as You know me! Holy Spirit, help me to increase my sensitivity to spiritual things. Help me to lay aside anything that is hindering my fellowship with the Father. Open my spiritual eyes and ears that I would see and hear from You. My heart's cry is that the reality of You would be more real to me. I pray that I would be so sensitive to Your Presence, that I not only hear Your voice, but I hear You walk into the room. My aim and utmost desire are to know You and Your power more than anyone has ever known before. Reveal Yourself to Me that I might know You more!

Chapter 17

THE EXPERIENCE OF GOD'S LOVE

And I have declared to them Your name, and will declare it, that the love with which You loved Me may be in them, and I in them (John 17:26).

If there ever was a crazy, out-of-this-world love relationship, it would be that of the Father and the Son. It is a simple and undebatable fact that God loves Jesus—and Jesus knows it!

This is a truth that is not talked about enough. Jesus had tremendous confidence in life and ministry because He not only knew His union with the Father, but He also knew how much God loved Him. We see this in the following verses:

> *The Father loves his Son so much that he has given all things into his hands* (John 3:35 TPT).

> *Because the Father loves his Son so much, he always reveals to him everything that he is about to do. And you will all be amazed when he shows him even greater works than what you've seen so far!* (John 5:20 TPT).

Look at what love will do! God loved Jesus so much that He not only gave all things to Jesus, but He also revealed all things to Jesus. God wasn't withholding! Jesus was able to boldly approach every situation in life because He knew God loved Him. It sounds a little weird because how is knowing God loves you going to help you stop a storm or raise the dead? It is because the love of God brings resources and revelation.

Jesus knew that because God loved Him, there would never be a situation He would face in which God would withhold the necessary resources and revelation to get the desired result. Would it be love to send one of your employees to do a job and not give them the necessary tools or tell them how to do the job? That is not love.

God loves Jesus. No one questions the love God has for Jesus, but how many of us have questioned the love God has for us? We have all been there at least once where we looked at the results of our lives and questioned the love of God. We know God loves Jesus, but when it comes to us, that's where the doubt sometimes comes. Well, let's settle that right now.

> *You live fully in me and now I live fully in them so that they will experience perfect unity, and the world will be convinced that you have sent me, for they will see that you love each one of them with the same passionate love that you have for me* (John 17:23 TPT).

We saw earlier that as Jesus was praying, He declared, "Father, the love You have for them is the same passionate love that You have for Me." It is an astounding statement to the carnal, unrenewed mind that God would love us as much as He loves Jesus. Believe me, I have been there many times. We automatically take a step back and began to analyze our actions, and the demons are always coming around trying to bring condemnation—but remember, this isn't about your actions; this is about your identity in Christ. Through salvation, Jesus made you the righteousness of God in Him. Jesus made you perfect just like Him!

I remember the first time I read that statement. I had a hard time believing it because I was looking at my body. I was looking at Chad in the flesh, not looking at Chad in the spirit. I had no revelation of what union truly produced at that point. However, the more I began to understand my union with Christ, the more I began to see myself the way God sees me (and I am still renewing my mind to it).

You need to settle with finality that God loves you in the exact way and to the same degree in which He loves Jesus! It will free you from condemnation and will give you boldness, knowing God's love for you also brings resources and revelation.

As Jesus concluded His prayer in the upper room, He then took the issue of the love of God to a higher level:

> *I have revealed to them who you are and i will continue to make you even more real to them, so that they may experience the same endless love that you have for me, for your love will now live in them, even as I live in them!* (John 17:26 TPT).

Remember, Jesus is praying this in the upper room with the eleven remaining disciples all hearing this. Can you imagine what they were thinking, hearing all these wonderful redemptive realities? Their minds must have been swirling with wonder and excitement! Jesus not only wanted them to know the love of God intellectually, but Jesus also wanted them to know the love of God experientially.

The more conscious you are of God, the more you will experience Him. Remember, the Christian experience is supposed to be an experience of Him! Look at God and Adam in the garden of Eden. God had put all things into Adam's hands and was revealing how things worked. God was walking and talking with Adam; God loved His creation. Unfortunately, Adam sinned and royally messed things up for thousands of years; however, Jesus came not only to fix things, but to make them better. Jesus came to reveal God's love for us by showing us God's love for Him. Jesus was showing us that what was available to Him would now be available to us. The resources Jesus had at His disposal would now be available to us. The revelation Jesus had at His disposal would now be available to us. Because of union, God would not be withholding!

> *Every spiritual blessing in the heavenly realm has already been lavished upon us as a love gift from our wonderful heavenly Father, the Father of our Lord Jesus—all*

*because he sees us wrapped into Christ. This
is why we celebrate him with all our hearts!*
(Ephesians 1:3 TPT).

God loves us so much that He gave us a love gift.
This gift was a massive present; it was an open door
to all of Heaven's resources! Anything and everything
we would need on the earth was made available to
us in Christ. If you need it, God made sure you had
access to it.

> *This is why the Scriptures say: Things never
> discovered or heard of before, things beyond
> our ability to imagine—these are the many
> things God has in store for all his lovers. But
> God now unveils these profound realities to
> us by the Spirit. Yes, he has revealed to us his
> inmost heart and deepest mysteries through
> the Holy Spirit, who constantly explores all
> things* (1 Corinthians 2:9–10 TPT).

I grew up hearing preachers talk about how we
were so unworthy and basically just stupid humans.
God's ways were so high and lofty that we couldn't

understand them; as a result, they just chalked up everything good or bad to the will of God—but this is not what God did!

God loves the Son and shows Him all things that He does. The love of God reveals so you can be a success for Him. God wants to have an intimate relationship with you, and there is no intimacy without the sharing of information and insights. Yes, God's ways are higher than our human ways, but He gave us the mind of Christ! God also gave us the Holy Spirit to reveal these profound realities to us so that we won't be in the dark.

God never created us to fulfill His plan on the earth and let us stumble around in the dark trying to figure things out on our own. Walking by faith is not walking around in a dark room, hoping I don't stump my toe. Walking by faith is walking in this dark world while living by the light of His love. God's love for Chad lights the way for Chad and provides everything Chad will need!

This love God has for you and me is also in us. God's love becomes part of our identity so that we can love others as He loves us. His love in us will not only compel us but enable us to reach out to the lost and hurting and manifest His supernatural grace and power to the world. How is this possible?

> *And I have declared to them Your name, and will declare it, that the love with which You loved Me may be in them, and I in them* (John 17:26).

As if Jesus hadn't mentioned it enough, this supernatural, prophetic prayer ends with these three powerful words: *I in them.* These three words perfectly summarize not only Jesus' prayer, but the gospel of Christ itself. The mystery of the gospel was "Christ in us." The cry of Jesus' heart was "I in them." The prayer of Jesus to the Father was "I in them." Jesus prayed for it, God heard it, and God fulfilled it. It is up to you and me as to whether we experience the fullness of it during our time on the earth.

PRAYER

Father, thank You for loving me. Thank You for loving me to the same degree that You love Jesus. I ask You to help me expand my mind to grasp this great love. Help me to understand the great magnitude of Your love for me and in me so that I walk in the fullness of You. Holy Spirit, open my eyes. Reveal to me the expansiveness of this extravagant love, that I would not only walk in this love for me, but I would walk in this love for others.

CONCLUSION

I in them and You in Me; that they would
be made perfect in One (John 17:23).

Union with Christ provided EVERYTHING. Union with Christ made me righteous, it gave me authority and dominion over the earth, it seated me with Him at God's right hand, it made me a master over disease and demons, it gave me access to all of Heaven's resources, it filled me with His life, and it made me to be like Him; most importantly, it put me in the position to know Him.

Union with Christ gave me eternal life not so I could just go to Heaven to be with Jesus, but so that I could be with Him and know Him now. If Jesus could have a relationship with the Father on the earth of seeing and hearing and knowing, so can you and me. Don't allow religion and the traditions of this world to cheat you out of your inheritance and your relationship with the Father.

Jesus united you with Him so you could live in Him and He could live through you. Everything Jesus prayed was not only true but has now come to pass. If you want to see what you are like, look at Jesus. If you want to see what is available, look at Jesus.

Jesus is not only the way to the Father, but Jesus is also the way of life, and there is no greater life than a life in Christ.

PRAYER

Father, I pray for wisdom and revelation in the knowledge of You. I pray the eyes of my soul would be enlightened so I could walk in a deeper intimacy with You. Help me to understand to a greater degree Your plan for my life, the inheritance You have in the saints, and the exceedingly great power in me that You used when You raised Jesus from the dead.

I ask for revelation of who I am in Christ so I would fully represent You on the earth. Help me to be heavenly minded. Show me in greater detail who I am as a sent one from Heaven. Give me greater insight and understanding of Your love for me so that Your life will fill my entire being and flow through me into the world.

Jesus, thank You for loving me. Thank You for setting me free. Thank You for uniting Yourself to me so we can work together in manifesting Heaven on the earth. Thank You for the privilege to know You—that You would be my very best friend and be more real to me than anything on the earth. I am eternally grateful, humbled, honored, and privileged to be one with You so that I can know You not only as the one true God, but also as my Father and best friend.

Endnotes

1. Greek Lexicon entry for Doxazo, *The King James Version New Testament Greek Lexicon* based on *Thayer's Greek Lexicon* and *Smith's Bible Dictionary*, https://www.biblestudytools.com/lexicons/greek/kjv/doxazo.html/.

2. G2222—zōē—*Strong's Greek Lexicon* (kjv). Blue Letter Bible. Accessed 23 Jul, 2022. https://www.blueletterbible.org/lexicon/g2222/kjv/tr/0-1/ss0/rl1/.

3. Greek Lexicon entry for Ginosko, *The NAS Testament Greek Lexicon* based on *Thayer's Greek Lexicon* and *Smith's Bible Dictionary,* https://www.biblestudytools.com/lexicons/greek/nas/ginosko.html/.

4. William Barclay, Commentary on John 17," *William Barclay' Daily Study Bible,* https://www.studylight.org/commentaries/eng/dsb/john-17.html/.

5. Tertullian, *Prescription Against Heretics*, chapter 36.

6. G5083—tēreō—*Strong's Greek Lexicon* (kjv). Blue Letter Bible. Accessed 12 Jul, 2022. https://www.blueletterbible.org/lexicon/g5083/kjv/tr/0-1/.

7. Greek Lexicon entry for Hagiazo, *The NAS Testament Greek Lexicon* based on *Thayer's Greek Lexicon* and

Smith's Bible Dictionary, https://www.biblestudytools.com/lexicons/greek/nas/hagiazo.html/.

8. Hebrew Lexicon entry for Kabowd, *The NAS Old Testament Hebrew Lexicon*, based on *Brown, Driver, Briggs Hebrew Lexicon,* https://www.biblestudytools.com/lexicons/hebrew/nas/kabowd.html.

9. Greek Lexicon entry for Doxa, *The NAS Testament Greek Lexicon* based on *Thayer's Greek Lexicon* and *Smith's Bible Dictionary,* https://www.biblestudytools.com/lexicons/greek/nas/doxa.html/.

10. Greek Lexicon entry for Emphanizo, *The NAS Testament Greek Lexicon* based on *Thayer's Greek Lexicon* and *Smith's Bible Dictionary,* https://www.biblestudytools.com/lexicons/greek/nas/emphanizo.html/.

ABOUT CHAD GONZALES

Dr. Chad Gonzales is the founder of *The Healing Academy*, host of *The Way Of Life* television program and *The Supernatural Life Podcast*. He holds a Master of Education and Doctorate of Ministry. Throughout the US and internationally, Chad has helped thousands experience miraculous healings; he is on a global mission to help the everyday believer walk according to the standard of Jesus Christ Himself.

YOUR Prophetic
COMMUNITY

Are you passionate about hearing God's voice, walking with Jesus, and experiencing the power of the Holy Spirit?

Destiny Image is a community of believers with a passion for equipping and encouraging you to live the prophetic, supernatural life you were created for!

We offer a fresh helping of practical articles, dynamic podcasts, and powerful videos from respected, Spirit-empowered, Christian leaders to fuel the holy fire within you.

Sign up now to get awesome content delivered to your inbox
destinyimage.com/sign-up

 Destiny Image